SURPRISE CHEFS

SURPRISE CHEFS

Kevin Woodford

NETWORK BOOKS

This book is published to accompany
the television series entitled *Surprise Chefs*
which was first broadcast in January 1996.
(The first series of *Surprise Chefs*
was broadcast in January 1994.)
The series is produced by Action Time UK Limited
for Meridian Broadcasting Limited

Network Books is an imprint of BBC Books,
a division of BBC Worldwide Publishing,
BBC Worldwide Limited, Woodlands,
80 Wood Lane, London W12 0TT

First published 1996
© Kevin Woodford 1996
The moral right of the author has been asserted

ISBN 0 563 38708 4

Designed by Sweeta Patel and Technical Art Services
Photographs by Philip Webb
Styling by Claire Louise Hunt
Home Economist: Sarah Ramsbottom

Set in Garamond
Printed in Great Britain by Martins of Berwick Ltd
Bound in Great Britain by Hunter and Foulis Ltd, Edinburgh
Colour separations by Radstock Reproductions Ltd, Midsomer Norton
Cover printed by Richard Clays Ltd, St Ives plc

I dedicate this book to Jean, Janine,
Steven and Mei-Wah

ACKNOWLEDGMENTS

I would like to record my thanks to Stephen Leahy, Chairman of Action Time UK Limited, for the inspiration and creation of *Surprise Chefs* and for his constant encouragement; to Mary McAnally, Director of Programmes, Meridian Broadcasting Limited, for the bold step in being the first to commission and broadcast not one, but three series of *Surprise Chefs*; to Bill Dale of Brookvale PR in the Isle of Man for his ability to read my writing and tolerate the pressure; to my copy-editor Susanna Tee for her attention to detail and sense of humour; and to Khadija Manjlai of BBC Books for her tenacity.

CONTENTS

INTRODUCTION

Keeping a well-stocked storecupboard and knowing how and when to buy good produce are key factors which will make cooking any day of the week a much simpler and more enjoyable task. There exist today huge supermarkets that have the facility to offer the shopper a vast range of products from all quarters of the world, often at affordable prices too, enabling us to be much more creative in the kitchen than ever before. Do remember, however, those super little delicatessen shops and market stalls that are often forsaken in our hurry to get the shopping out of the way as quickly as possible. There are often lots of goodies just waiting round the corner.

STORECUPBOARD INGREDIENTS

It's a prudent cook who keeps a few basic essentials in the larder – but I do mean essentials. It's only too easy to think 'you never know when I might want one of those...' and into the larder it goes. This is the 'shortage syndrome' brought about by the occasional dearth of something like sugar or a famine (although this hasn't happened for decades, you never know when it might...), so it's better to be safe than sorry.

Now is the time to revise your thinking. The reality is, you usually use only the last things in – so the rest gets older and older, cans get rustier and bags split. Cans may seem as if they last for ever – but whilst the contents are still edible, there is something less than appealing about a dented can of mushy peas with the price in old money on it. A bit of ruthless action is needed.

The best storecupboard contains staples for everyday meals, plus a few luxuries for emergencies when unexpected guests start looking hungry. Here is a storecupboard guide list.

STAPLES
FISH
These are *always* useful – and very good canned. Often they bear no resemblance to the fresh version, but are nevertheless a treat in their own right
Tuna – for salads, pasta and sandwiches
Sardines – sandwiches, pizza toppings

Pilchards – one of the cheapest forms. Use like the above fish and also in casseroles with potatoes, or with salads

Anchovies – essential for pizza toppings and salads like Niçoise, also for adding a delicious salty savouriness to beef stews or puddings

MEAT
Corned beef
Canned ham

VEGETABLES AND PULSES
Chopped tomatoes – every cook's right-hand man. Use in everything from goulash to chicken casserole, from pizza toppings to chilli con carne
Instant mash – to be enhanced with grated onion, cheese, etc.
Chickpeas – canned or dried
Baked beans

FRUIT
Canned or dried are always useful for baking and desserts
Pineapple – canned
Apricots – canned and dried
Sultanas
Seedless raisins
Glacé cherries

NUTS
Flaked almonds – for salads and cakes
Ground almonds – for baking and curries
Peanut butter – a kids' tea standby – useful for satay sauces too

PASTA
Spaghetti
Lasagna
Noodles
Penne or shells – for salads

RICE
Easy-cook long grain
Risotto rice – for risottos and paella

FLOUR AND CEREALS
Plain and self-raising
Wholemeal
Cornflour

Oats
Breakfast cereals

SUGAR AND SYRUP
Granulated sugar
Caster sugar
Brown sugar
Icing sugar

HERBS
These are best bought fresh. There are just a few to keep in the larder – but remember they deteriorate fast.
Bouquet garni
Thyme
Rosemary
Tarragon
Bay leaves
Oregano

SPICES
Keep these in airtight, opaque containers in small amounts – the flavours disappear quickly.
Black and white peppercorns
Paprika
Cayenne
Chilli powder
Ground coriander
Turmeric
Cinnamon sticks or ground cinnamon
Caraway seeds
Nutmeg
Vanilla

OILS
Sunflower oil
Olive oil

VINEGARS
Red and white wine vinegar
Malt vinegar

SAUCES AND FLAVOURINGS
Pesto
Worcestershire sauce
Tabasco sauce
Soy sauce
Tomato sauce
Canned or packet custard
English mustard
Dijon mustard
Wholegrain mustard

STOCK CUBES
All flavours

RELISHES AND PRESERVES
Mango chutney
Piccalilli
Jams
Clear honey

DRINKS
Instant and ground coffee
Teas
Cocoa powder

LUXURIES
For special occasions, canned salmon, artichoke hearts, asparagus, petits pois, lychees, figs and mangoes are worth remembering. Flageolet beans add a lovely French feel to lamb dishes. Special oils include walnut or hazelnut and for posh vinegars, choose tarragon, sherry or balsamic.

SHOPPING

Never go shopping on an empty stomach – it's fatal. You end up spending a mint on a heap of things which will be relegated to – yes, the storecupboard.

We are not all list makers, in fact few cooks are organized at all, leaving a lot to inspiration and instinct. Making a shopping list, however, is seriously the most sensible way of shopping.

Shopping daily and locally brings out the thrifty side of you as one tends to buy only what is needed – and it all fits into one carrier bag. And this means you can take advantage of local markets where fresh fruit and vegetables are definitely cheaper.

Those who favour the once-a-week supermarket shop might think list-making is a daunting and unnecessary task when it's probably difficult enough to find the time to do the shopping in the first place. But it isn't. It's good discipline and saves money, even if the list is five yards long. This does not mean you are denied the spontaneous purchase of something on special offer, or a new fruit or vegetable, for example. Just swap it for something already on the list.

Regular supermarket shoppers will know their way around their own store so make the list in order so you don't keep retracing your steps up and down the aisles.

Most supermarkets have fresh fruit and vegetables at the entrance. This is always colourful, stimulating, fragrant and exciting, particularly considering how privileged we are to be able to try strange and delicious produce from all over the world.

Though there are always pre-packed fruit and vegetables on offer, it is probably more sensible to select your own. This way you can have less in weight than a prepacked amount and you can examine each item for any flaws or damage.

Be adventurous with your choice. Tomatoes, for example, range from tiny cherries, to huge beefsteaks with everything in between. Mushrooms aren't just mushrooms any more. Tiny buttons are great for salads, whilst big flat field mushrooms add colour and taste to stews and casseroles. Shiitake and Oysters are perfect for oriental-style dishes – and they all taste different.

Choose fresh vegetables carefully and weigh them. Supermarkets always provide scales for you to check. Inspect pre-packed vegetables for any signs of mould or sweating at the bottom of the pack. And *always* look at the sell-by date.

You will need fruit for eating on its own and also for use in cooking. Sometimes one particular variety of apple is cheaper because it is on promotion. Try these as they may turn out to be the best you have ever eaten.

Don't be put off by some of the strange-looking fruits which are now common here. Most supermarkets display product information to tell you what they taste like and suggestions for how to use them.

Citrus fruits are a major source of Vitamin C. But don't just stick to plain old oranges. Throughout the year there are a range of newly developed ones such as mineolas as well as the seasonal varieties like mandarin and clementines. Grapefruits are no longer sour – just try a Ruby. They are deliciously fashionable and not just for breakfast. They go equally well with rich meats such as duck or pork for dinner party dishes.

The meat you buy usually has the star role in a meal. There is a massive range of top quality meat available from mince to quails, although I have never quite seen the point of quails. Chicken includes corn-fed free range and they come in all sizes. They also come in prepared joints which makes midweek cookery a doddle. These are always fast to cook to make fantastic, tempting flavoursome meals all the family will enjoy.

Some supermarkets have a fresh meat counter and this is where you will find the more unusual items like game or one slice of steak. Another tip for midweek cooking is to look out for speciality sausages. These designer types have lifted the reputation of the humble banger into the gourmet class.

Fish counters are often a really pleasing sight. A brilliant array of gleaming fish always tempts me to have some for supper. The fish is usually of superlative quality – supermarkets couldn't afford for it to be otherwise. As a check, eyes should be bright and the skin of mackerel, salmon, trout and sardines should be moist and gleaming. Fillets of cod and haddock, for example, should have tightly packed flakes and attractive translucency. However, don't let this put you off buying ready-frozen fish for the freezer. Fish should be cooked and eaten on the same day it is purchased for the best results. If you are buying on Monday for the week with fish featuring on Friday, choose frozen.

On the subject of freezers, what are they really for? In reality they are a very helpful and rather sophisticated cupboard but fresh food is usually best.

The most useful items to buy for the freezer are fish, minced beef, fish fingers for children, frozen peas and possibly ice-cream and *always* frozen puff pastry. Sliced bread is also a brilliant freezer standby and can be toasted from frozen. In any case, it only takes minutes for single slices to thaw for sandwiches. A pack of butter, a carton of milk and even an emergency packet of pre-packed bacon will get you out of trouble on many occasions when the shops are shut.

I haven't mentioned eggs. Always look at the sell-by date on egg boxes. Eggs will keep fresh for 3 weeks if kept in the fridge but, obviously, they taste better at the beginning of the 3 weeks than at the tail end.

Buy bread daily unless you are keeping sliced loaves in the freezer. You can really only get one day out of a loaf.

To get back to the list at the beginning which you are now all going to make, the other and very important thing to remember is – menu planning. Don't groan.

Seasonal produce is always at its best and cheapest. Even though many fruits and vegetables which used to be seasonal are now available, imported, year-round, they are expensive.

Sometimes menus need special ingredients, such as paprika for goulash, coconut milk for Thai-style curries, sun-dried tomato paste for a sun-soaked south-of-France dish. *Always* check in the larder to make sure you need to buy it. This way you avoid a platoon of Worcestershire sauce lining up reproachfully every time you open the larder door.

All this advice applies to daily shoppers as well as the supermarket shopper.

Finally – wine. You can be confident about buying wine in the supermarket at the same time as you do your food shopping. It is always value for money and invariably cheaper. Furthermore, there are always special offers, wines of the month, discounts and advice on matching wine with foods. Buying in bulk means huge savings and you will usually find a carry-out service to transport a whole case to your car.

ABOUT THE RECIPES

Here are a few points to note about the recipes.

Most recipes are designed to serve 4 people,
unless otherwise specified.

Spoon measurements are level.

Size 3 eggs are used for the recipes, unless otherwise specified.

Ovens vary considerably, so adjust cooking times,
if necessary, to suit your particular oven.

Taste as you cook, and adjust seasoning
to suit your own personal preference.

Wash fruits and vegetables before you prepare them.

Where herbs are listed as chopped or snipped,
fresh herbs are best. If you do use dried herbs,
use only half the quantity.

STARTERS

T he simplest of ingredients can become a tantalizing first course with just a little imagination. In my opinion there are two approaches to concocting starters, a theory which could be applied to most sections of this book but particularly so for this chapter.

One is to plan carefully the dish and, in so doing, relate the ingredients and style of cooking to the guests and the occasion and then go out in search of those specific ingredients. The other is simply to create a starter from whatever the contents of your refrigerator and storecupboard afford. This often involves the use of dressings which is why it is always a good idea to stock a range of interesting and varied oils and vinegars.

Many of the recipes which feature in this chapter could quite easily be served as snacks without the need to change the recipe at all. I must confess that, not being the greediest of diners, I actually prefer to eat two starters as opposed to one starter and a main course.

Cinnamon-glazed Grapefruit

Grapefruit is one of the very few citrus fruits which can benefit from being heated. Its abundance of juice ensures that it will remain moist and not lose its flavour.
The dish benefits from the fruit being prepared several hours prior to grilling it so that the additional ingredients have time to penetrate into the juicy segments. It should be served immediately after grilling.

Serves 4

2 large grapefruits
50 g (2 oz) soft brown sugar
1 teaspoon ground cinnamon

4 tablespoons sherry
4 mint leaves, to garnish

Cut the grapefruit in half and cut around each half, loosening the flesh from the outer skin. Carefully remove the central pith then loosen each segment by cutting between the flesh and the membranes.

Mix together the sugar and cinnamon. Pour the sherry over the flesh of the fruit and top with the sugar mixture. Leave to soak for at least 2 hours.

To serve, place under a hot grill until golden brown. Garnish with mint leaves.

Pizza Spago

I love this recipe – it's such a light, tasty dish and so easy to make. It makes a perfect starter for a light supper or even dinner party. Spago is another of those dishes which will adapt to other ingredients being added – black olives, anchovies, capers, prosciutto ham, in fact whatever you fancy really.

Makes 4

½ quantity of Pizza dough
  (page 32)
Juice of ½ a lemon
3 tablespoons chopped fresh dill
2 garlic cloves, crushed
100 g (4 oz) butter

50 g (2 oz) onion, finely sliced
100 g (4 oz) full-fat soft cheese
50 g (2 oz) smoked salmon,
  finely diced
Salt and freshly ground black pepper

Prepare the pizza dough as described in the recipe on page 32. Put the dough in a bowl, cover with a clean tea-towel and leave in a warm place for 25 minutes until doubled in size.

Pre-heat the oven to 200°C/400°F/Gas 6. Turn the dough onto a lightly floured surface and knead for 1–2 minutes to knock out the air. Cut the dough into 4 pieces and roll out each piece to a thin round. Prick each with a fork to prevent excessive rising during baking.

Mix together the lemon juice, 1 tablespoon of dill, garlic and butter and spread over the pizza bases. Place a layer of sliced onion on top. Bake for 10–15 minutes until the dough is cooked.

Mix together the cheese, smoked salmon and remaining dill and season with salt and pepper. Spread this mixture over the pizzas and serve immediately.

Devilled Chicken Livers on a Timbale of Pilaff Rice

❦

Classically, chicken livers have always been served slightly undercooked but it should be noted that it is far safer to cook them fully.

Serves 4

65 g (2½ oz) butter
50 g (2 oz) onion, finely chopped
150 ml (5 fl oz) patna rice
(measured in a jug)
300 ml (10 fl oz) hot chicken stock
1 bay leaf
1 tablespoon walnut oil
225 g (8 oz) chicken livers
¼ teaspoon cayenne pepper
1 tablespoon bottled, preserved pink and green peppercorns
50 g (2 oz) shallots, finely chopped

1 garlic clove, crushed
25 g (1 oz) snipped fresh chives
1 teaspoon crushed black peppercorns
1 tablespoon mustard
75 g (3 oz) tomatoes, seeded and chopped
3 tablespoons brandy
150 ml (5 fl oz) gravy (left over from the Sunday roast)
1 drop of Tabasco sauce
Salt and freshly ground black pepper

First prepare the rice pilaff. Melt 15 g (½ oz) of the butter in a pan, add the onion and cook for 2–3 minutes. Stir in the rice then add the stock. Season lightly with salt and pepper and add the bay leaf. Cover and cook gently for 10–15 minutes until the stock has been absorbed and the rice is tender but moist. Remove the bay leaf and, using a fork, add the remaining 50 g (2 oz) butter, being careful not to break up the rice. Check and, if necessary, adjust the seasoning. Cover and keep warm.

Heat the walnut oil in a pan, add the livers and season with salt and cayenne pepper. Cook for 2–3 minutes until sealed and fully cooked then remove from the pan. Add the pink and green peppercorns, the shallots, garlic, chives, black peppercorns, mustard and tomatoes to the pan. Cook for about 1–2 minutes then add the brandy. Ignite to burn off the alcohol then add the gravy and the Tabasco sauce.

Add the livers to the sauce. Check and, if necessary, adjust the seasoning. Place the rice into a small, lightly greased ring mould and turn out onto serving plates. Place the livers in the centre and serve.

Chilled Cream of Watercress and Almond Soup

There are not many soups that I can honestly say I enjoy when served chilled but this one, on a sunny day, is a sheer delight. As with most chilled soups, this is also good when served hot.

Serves 4

50 g (2 oz) butter
25 g (1 oz) flaked almonds
450 g (1 lb) leeks, white parts only, thinly sliced
3 bunches watercress, stalks removed and leaves chopped
3 potatoes, peeled and chopped
900 ml (1½ pints) chicken stock

1 tablespoon chopped fresh chervil
1 bay leaf
150 ml (5 fl oz) double cream
Salt and freshly ground black pepper
25 g (1 oz) flaked almonds, toasted, to garnish
4 sprigs of watercress, to garnish

Melt the butter in a pan. Add the flaked almonds, then the leeks and cook for 2 minutes. Add the watercress and potatoes and cook for a further 15 minutes, stirring frequently to prevent burning.

Pour in the stock, add the chervil and bay leaf and simmer for 20 minutes. Season with salt and pepper to taste and cool slightly. Remove the bay leaf and purée the soup in a food processor. Blend in the cream, taste and, if necessary, adjust the seasoning.

Leave the soup to chill. Serve garnished with toasted flaked almonds and a sprig of watercress.

Cream of Celery and Apple Soup

❦

This is basically a simple puréed vegetable soup, with a raw apple garnish. Its virtue lies in its subtle combination of ingredients. Use the strongest most mature Cheddar you can find or the flavour of the cheese will be swamped. The same holds true for the apples; choose a tart eating variety with a lot of crunch like Cox's Orange Pippin. Although the parsley could be optional, the soup is a bit drab in colour without it and really does need a touch of green. The soup can be made in advance and heated gently just before you serve it. However, don't let it boil when you reheat it or the cheese will become rubbery.

Serves 4

50 g (2 oz) butter
1 large leek, thinly sliced
1 medium onion, chopped
6–8 celery stalks, sliced
1.6 litres (2¾ pints) hot chicken stock
100 g (4 oz) strong Cheddar cheese, grated
50 ml (2 fl oz) single cream
1 medium eating apple
4 teaspoons horseradish cream
1 tablespoon finely chopped fresh parsley
Salt and freshly ground black pepper

Put the butter in a heavy-based pan and melt over medium heat until it foams. Add the leek, onion and celery, cover and cook for about 5 minutes until the vegetables are softened but not brown.

Pour in the hot stock, cover the pan and turn the heat up to high. When the soup boils, turn the heat down to low and simmer, covered, for 45 minutes. Using a spoon, skim the top of the soup to remove any floating scum or fat.

Purée the soup in a food processor or rub through a sieve. Pour into a clean pan, bring to the boil and season with salt and pepper to taste. Add the grated cheese and stir. The cheese need not melt completely. Add the cream and mix well.

Peel and finely chop the apple, then place a spoonful in the bottom of 4 individual bowls. Pour in the soup and drop 1 teaspoon horseradish cream into the centre. Depending on the heaviness of your horseradish, you could try using the tip of a knife to draw it out in lines from the middle to create a classy effect. Sprinkle over the parsley and serve immediately.

Comice Pear with a Smoked Ham and Tarragon Dressing

This unusual starter can be made well in advance of a dinner party and it will retain all its original qualities. For very special occasions I change the ham and use smoked salmon and add a teaspoon of lemon juice.

Serves 4

4 Comice pears
150 ml (5 fl oz) tarragon vinegar
1 tablespoon chopped fresh dill
10 tarragon leaves
150 ml (5 fl oz) white wine vinegar
1 teaspoon chopped fresh tarragon

Juice of 1¼ lemons
Pinch of caster sugar
75 g (3 oz) smoked ham, diced
2 tablespoons crème fraîche
1 tablespoon finely chopped shallots
Salt and freshly ground black pepper

Peel the pears without removing the stalks. Place in a wide saucepan, add the tarragon vinegar, dill and 6 of the tarragon leaves. Cover with a little cold water and season with salt and pepper. Poach gently over a low heat for about 15 minutes until tender. Leave the pears in the cooking liquid until cold.

Using a small knife, slice across the bottom of each pear so that it will sit neatly on a plate. Carefully remove the core from the base of the pears to form a cavity inside.

Mix together the white wine vinegar, chopped tarragon, juice of 1 lemon and the caster sugar. Mix together the ham, crème fraîche, remaining juice of a ¼ lemon and the shallots. Season with salt and pepper. Use this mixture to fill the insides of the pears. Sit the pears on 4 individual plates and surround with the dressing. Garnish the pears with the remaining tarragon leaves.

Herrings pickled in a Lemon Thyme Marinade

Freshly pickled herrings are lovely all year round. They are one of the few items for which I would forsake seasons. I like to serve a warm potato salad with this dish.

Makes 8

FOR THE MARINADE:
600 ml (1 pint) white wine vinegar
150 ml (¼ pint) dry white wine
50 g (2 oz) onion, thinly sliced
Pinch of salt
6 chillies
2 bay leaves
25 g (1 oz) fresh lemon thyme
4 black peppercorns
4 white peppercorns
Juice 1 of lemon

2 tablespoons chopped fresh parsley
1 small garlic clove, crushed
Pinch of allspice
3 cloves

TO FINISH:
8 herring fillets
8 sprigs of lemon thyme
8 large gherkins
75 g (3 oz) red pepper, finely sliced
Salt

Put all the marinade ingredients into a pan, bring to the boil, simmer gently for 2 minutes then leave to cool.

Lay the herrings flat in a dish, cover with salt and chill for 12 hours. Wash off all the salt under cold slow-running water for at least 1 hour.

Place a sprig of thyme on the inside of each herring then top with a gherkin and some red pepper. Roll up and secure with a cocktail stick. Place in a bowl.

Strain the cold marinade over the herrings, cover and store in the fridge for 3 days before serving.

Duck Liver Pâté with a Hot Citrus Salad

❧❀❧

A rich pâté which many would say is a meal in itself.

Serves 8

450 g (1 lb) ducks' liver, ducts
    removed
1 tablespoon chopped fresh mixed
    herbs
1 garlic clove, crushed
50 g (2 oz) shallots, finely chopped
4 tablespoons sherry
350 g (13 oz) butter
6 tablespoons brandy

2 oranges, segmented
3 limes, segmented
2 lemons, segmented
Grated rind of 2 oranges
Grated rind of 1 lemon
50 g (2 oz) demerara sugar
1 tablespoon chopped fresh mint
Salt and freshly ground black pepper

Put the livers, mixed herbs, garlic and shallots in a bowl and add the sherry. Leave to marinade for 2 hours.

Drain off the juice and retain. Heat 50 g (2 oz) of the butter in a frying pan, add the liver mixture and season with salt and pepper. Cook for 3–5 minutes. Do not overcook the liver, they should be pink. Add the marinade liquid and 3 tablespoons of the brandy, then burn off the alcohol by setting alight. Be careful when doing this.

Purée the mixture in a food processor. Add 250 g (9 oz) of the butter and mix together. Check and adjust the seasoning if necessary.

Pack the pâté into a terrine dish lined with cling film, and chill.

Just before serving, put the fruit segments and the remaining 50 g (2 oz) of the butter into a pan and heat for 1 minute. Add the orange and lemon rind and the sugar, cook for a further 2 minutes then pour in the remaining 3 tablespoons of brandy and flame. Finally, add the mint. Serve a slice of the pâté with the hot citrus salad.

Asparagus and Oyster Mushrooms with a Chive Couscous

❦

There's a certain freshness to this recipe which I never tire of and, for me, the combination of asparagus and oyster mushrooms remains an earthy one. It's interesting to note that my hostage for this dish had a packet of couscous on the shelf and was oblivious as to what to do with it. Couscous is of North African origin and is produced as small pellets from semolina.

Serves 4

75 g (3 oz) couscous
300 ml (10 fl oz) chicken stock
50 ml (2 fl oz) water
175 ml (6 fl oz) dry white wine
4 tablespoons sherry
2 bunches of asparagus, trimmed
½ garlic clove, crushed
Pinch of paprika

Juice of 1 lemon
75 g (3 oz) oyster mushrooms, sliced
1 tablespoon snipped fresh chives
100 ml (4 fl oz) double cream
50 g (2 oz) butter
2 tomatoes, seeded and chopped
12 coriander leaves
Salt and freshly ground black pepper

Put the couscous in a bowl, add the chicken stock and stir together. Put the water, wine and sherry in a frying pan, add the asparagus, garlic, paprika and lemon juice and simmer gently for 5 minutes. Add the mushrooms, season lightly with salt and pepper and cook for 2 minutes.

Meanwhile, season the couscous with salt and pepper, add the chives and mix together. Place the couscous into 4 lightly oiled dariole or ramekin dishes. Cover with kitchen foil and place in a pan containing enough water to come a quarter way up the dishes. Cook over a medium heat for 8–10 minutes to heat through.

Meanwhile, remove the asparagus and mushrooms from the pan, cover and keep warm. Boil the cooking liquid until reduced by half, then stir in the cream. Reduce the heat and whisk in the butter. Check and, if necessary, adjust the seasoning. Return the asparagus and mushrooms to the sauce and remove from the heat.

Using a knife, loosen the couscous from the edges of the dishes and invert onto an oval plate covering the top third of the plate area. Neatly arrange the asparagus and mushrooms on the remainder of the plate and spoon over the sauce. Place 3 small spoonfuls of tomato flesh around the plate and top with coriander leaves.

Avocado and Capsicum Salad

The avocado for this dish needs to be ripe but not soft. It's worth buying them underripe and allowing them to ripen under your own guidance. That way you will be sure that it is perfect when eaten.

Serves 2

1 ripe avocado
1 red pepper, seeded and thinly sliced
1 green pepper, seeded and thinly sliced
50 g (2 oz) shallots, finely chopped
50 g (2 oz) young spinach leaves, chopped

2 tablespoons chopped fresh coriander
Juice of 1 lemon
100 ml (4 fl oz) natural yoghurt
Pinch of cayenne pepper
Salt and freshly ground black pepper

Halve the avocado, remove the stone and peel. Slice into thick pieces.

Mix the avocado, peppers and shallots with the spinach leaves and half of the coriander. Toss in most of the lemon juice and season with cayenne pepper, salt and pepper. Transfer the salad to a dish.

Season the yoghurt with a little salt and pepper. Add a little lemon juice and the remaining coriander. Pour the dressing down the centre of the salad and serve.

Avocado baked with Stilton accompanied by a Celery and Apple Sauce

❧❀❧

Avocado has the ability to take on flavours from other ingredients whilst retaining its own characteristics, particularly so in this recipe.

Serves 4

2 ripe avocados
75 g (3 oz) Stilton
25 g (1 oz) celery, finely chopped
25 g (1 oz) apple, finely chopped
25 g (1 oz) broken walnuts, chopped
50 ml (2 fl oz) double cream
1 egg yolk
50 g (1 oz) fine soft breadcrumbs
Salt and freshly ground black pepper

FOR THE SAUCE:
75 g (3 oz) apple
25 g (1 oz) butter
75 g (3 oz) celery, finely chopped
50 g (2 oz) leek, finely chopped
250 ml (8 fl oz) natural yoghurt
50 ml (2 fl oz) cream
1 tablespoon lemon juice
Pinch of cayenne pepper
Salt and freshly ground black pepper

Pre-heat the oven to 190°C/375°F/Gas 5.

Cut the avocados in half and remove the flesh, reserving the shells. Purée in a food processor with the Stilton, celery, apple and walnuts. Season with salt and pepper to taste and carefully beat in the cream and egg yolk, taking care not to curdle the mixture.

Return mixture to the avocado shells and sprinkle with the breadcrumbs. Bake for 15 mintues until golden brown.

Meanwhile, prepare the sauce. Finely chop the apple. Melt the butter in a pan, add the apple, celery and leek and cook for 2–3 minutes until softened slightly. Add the yoghurt, cream and lemon juice, and season with cayenne, salt and pepper. Heat gently then pour into a sauceboat or jug and serve with the avocados.

A Hot Mousse of Smoked Herring

Any smoked fish will work in this easy-to-follow recipe, but my favourite,
without doubt, is smoked herring. I like to serve it with a crisp salad
consisting of as many varied salad leaves as are available lightly dressed with
a lemon and walnut oil vinaigrette.

Serves 4–6

---

175 g (6 oz) smoked herrings
Juice of ½ a lemon
Pinch of paprika
1 size 6 egg white
175 ml (6 fl oz) double cream

1 tablespoon snipped fresh chives
1 tablespoon chopped fresh coriander
Freshly ground black pepper
Hot buttered toast or brown bread
 and butter, to serve

Pre-heat the oven to 160°C/325°C/Gas 3.

Remove the skin and bones from the herrings. Purée the flesh in a food
processor. Add the lemon juice and paprika, then gradually add the egg white
whilst the machine is on high speed. Reduce the speed and carefully add the
cream, watching to ensure that the mixture does not curdle. Once the mixture has been fully blended, turn off the machine, add the pepper and herbs
and mix in.

Transfer the mixture to 4–6 individual ramekin dishes and place them in a
roasting dish containing a little hot water. Bake for 8–12 minutes until firm.

Serve with brown bread and butter or, even better still, hot buttered toast.

Turnip, Fennel and Orange Soup

This soup was created purely from the ingredients in a shopper's trolley with nothing removed and nothing added. The result, for all involved, was a resounding success.

Serves 4

125 g (5 oz) butter
225 g (8 oz) onions, chopped
350 g (12 oz) potatoes, chopped
450 g (1 lb) turnips, chopped
100 g (4 oz) fennel, sliced
Grated rind and juice of 1 orange

1.5 litres (2½ pints) chicken or
*   vegetable stock*
300 ml (½ pint) milk
1 bouquet garni
50 ml (2 fl oz) double cream
Salt and freshly ground black pepper

Melt 75 g (3 oz) of the butter in a deep pan, add the onions and cook for 5 minutes without browning. Add the potatoes, turnips and fennel and cook for a further 5–8 minutes until slightly softened. Add the orange rind and juice, stock and milk and bring slowly to the boil. Add the bouquet garni and simmer for 45 minutes.

Remove the bouquet garni and purée the soup in a food processor until smooth. Return to the heat, add the cream and whisk in the remaining 50 g (2 oz) of butter.

Check and, if necessary, adjust the seasoning and consistency. If too thick, add a little more milk or stock. If too thin, then reduce the soup by boiling for a moment or two.

Mulligatawny with Garlic Croûtons

❦

This can be tailor-made cookery. If you like your food hot and spicy then simply increase the amount of curry powder. The garlic croûtons add texture to the soup.

Serves 4

150 g (6 oz) butter
100 g (4 oz) onions, finely chopped
50 g (2 oz) celery, finely chopped
50 g (2 oz) leeks, finely chopped
50 g (2 oz) carrots, finely chopped
50 g (2 oz) plain flour
10 g (½ oz) curry powder
1 tablespoon tomato purée
50 g (2 oz) apple, finely chopped
25 g (1 oz) mango chutney

1.75 litres (3 pints) chicken stock
1 bouquet garni
50 ml (2 fl oz) double cream
10 g (½ oz) long-grain rice, cooked
2 garlic cloves, crushed
1 tablespoon chopped fresh parsley
3 slices white bread, crusts removed
  and cubed
Salt and freshly ground black pepper

Heat 50 g (2 oz) of the butter in a pan, add the onions, celery, leeks and carrots and cook for 5 minutes. Add the flour and curry powder and cook for 2 minutes, stirring.

Add the tomato purée, apple and mango chutney. Mix together and pour in the stock. Add the bouquet garni, bring to the boil and simmer for 45 minutes. When cooked, remove the bouquet garni, season with salt and pepper, and add the cream and rice.

Melt the remaining 100 g (4 oz) of butter. When hot, add the garlic and parsley. Cook for 1 minute then add the bread cubes. Cook until golden brown. Serve the soup with the croûtons sprinkled on top.

Glazed Mushrooms stuffed with a Coriander Duxelle

⋅⋙⋘⋅

This colourful mushroom dish can be served as a starter, snack or accompaniment to a main dish.

Serves 4

8 large flat mushrooms
Juice of 1 lemon
1 tablespoon plain flour
150 g (6 oz) unsalted butter
100 g (4 oz) button mushrooms, finely chopped
75 g (3 oz) shallots, finely chopped
1 garlic clove, crushed
2 tablespoons chopped fresh coriander

40 g (1½ oz) fresh white breadcrumbs
2 tomatoes, skinned, seeded and finely chopped
1 tablespoon white wine
2 egg yolks
1 tablespoon chopped fresh tarragon
Salt and freshly ground black pepper
Mixed dressed salad leaves, to garnish

Remove the stalks from the flat mushrooms, chop and set aside.

In a small pan of boiling water, whisk ½ the lemon juice and the flour. Add the flat mushrooms and simmer for about 5 minutes until tender. (The lemon and flour mixture will help to keep their colour.)

Melt 50 g (2 oz) of the butter in a pan and add the chopped mushrooms, chopped stalks, shallots, garlic and coriander. Cook for 3–4 minutes until softened then add the breadcrumbs and tomatoes. Season with salt and pepper. Remove from the heat.

Drain the large mushrooms and carefully dry them. Gently melt the remaining 100 g (4 oz) of butter. Whisk the white wine and the egg yolks, in a bowl, over a pan of boiling water until they become light and fluffy. Gradually whisk in the melted butter. Add the tarragon and the remaining lemon juice and season with salt and pepper to taste.

Fill the large mushrooms with the duxelle and top with the sauce. Cook the mushrooms under a hot grill until brown and glazed. Serve garnished with dressed salad leaves.

Caramelized Tartlet of Pear and Leek

❧❀❧

This unusual combination of ingredients yields a delicious surprise. The leeks take on a sweetness from the orange juice and will have your friends guessing as to what they are.

Makes 4

75 g (3 oz) plain white flour
40 g (1½ oz) wholemeal flour
65 g (2½ oz) margarine
20 g (¾ oz) clear honey
50 g (2 oz) baby leeks, finely chopped
Grated rind and juice of ½ an orange

2 firm pears
2 eggs
150 ml (5 fl oz) double cream
15 g (½ oz) caster sugar
65 g (2½ oz) demerara sugar
Freshly ground black pepper

Pre-heat the oven to 190°C/375°F/Gas 5.

Sift the white flour into a bowl and add the wholemeal flour. Add the margarine and rub in until the mixture resembles breadcrumbs. Add the honey and mix together to form a dough. On a lightly floured surface, roll out the dough and use to line 4 individual Yorkshire pudding moulds. Prick the pastry and bake in the oven for 12–15 minutes until golden brown. Leave to cool.

Meanwhile, put the leeks, orange rind and juice in a pan and cook for 5 minutes until tender. Leave to cool. Core, peel and thinly slice the pears. Whisk together the eggs, cream, both the caster and demerara sugar and pour into a jug.

Fill the pastry cases with the leeks and season lightly with pepper. Arrange the pear slices on top and pour over the cream mixture. Cook in the oven for about 15 minutes until the custard has set.

LIGHT SNACKS

I believe that the basis for good snacks lies in the theory of the recipes having been developed under the heading of comfort food. A light snack should not only satisfy one's hunger but should also lift the spirit. I hope you will find the recipes in this chapter do just that.

Pissaladière

This is a classical Mediterranean recipe, drawing on all of the full flavours to be found around the south of France into Italy. This, along with a glass of chilled white or rosé wine, leaves little to be desired.

Serves 4

FOR THE PIZZA DOUGH:
225 g (8 oz) plain flour
1 teaspoon salt
1½ teaspoons dried yeast
100 ml (4 fl oz) water, hand hot
¼ teaspoon caster sugar
1 egg, beaten
1 teaspoon olive oil

FOR THE FILLING:
5 tablespoons olive oil
1.25 kg (2½ lb) medium onions,
* sliced*
2 garlic cloves, crushed
75 g (3 oz) anchovy fillets
100 g (4 oz) stoned black olives
1 tablespoon Herbes de Provence, or
* mixed chopped fresh herbs*
1 tablespoon chopped fresh parsley
Salt and freshly ground black pepper

Sift the flour and salt into a bowl and make a hollow in the centre. Sprinkle the yeast into 75 ml (3 fl oz) of the water and whisk in the sugar. Leave in a warm place for 15 minutes until frothy.

Pour the yeast mixture into the flour, add the beaten egg and mix to form a soft dough. If necessary, use the remaining 25 ml (1 fl oz) of water if the dough feels too dry.

Grease a baking tray measuring 33 x 23 cm (13 x 9 in). On a lightly floured surface, knead the dough for 10 minutes until it feels springy and smooth. Roll out the dough to fit the baking tray. Transfer it to the tray, ensuring that the dough is squeezed into the corners. Brush the dough with 1 teaspoon of olive oil. Cover with a clean tea-towel and leave in a warm place for 25 minutes until doubled in size.

To make the filling, heat the olive oil in a pan, add the onions and garlic and cook for 10 minutes until soft and golden brown. Season with salt and pepper then add the oil from the anchovies. Pre-heat the oven to 200°C/400°F/Gas 6. Spread the onions over the dough base. Cut the anchovies in half lengthways and arrange trellis-fashion over the onions. Place the olives in the gaps and sprinkle with the Herbes de Provence. Bake in the oven for about 20 minutes until golden brown. Sprinkle the chopped parsley on top before serving.

Cheese and Paprika Sticks

❦

These are lovely when served straight from the oven. They're ideal as an appetizer prior to a meal or simply as a snack on their own.

Makes about 20

50 g (2 oz) plain flour	25 g (1 oz) freshly grated Parmesan
1 tablespoon paprika	1 tablespoon snipped fresh chives
Pinch of salt	1 egg yolk
25 g (1 oz) butter, softened	

Sift together the flour, paprika and salt into a bowl. Rub in the butter until the mixture resembles breadcrumbs then add the cheese and chives. Mix in the egg yolk and a little water, if needed, to form a smooth dough. Chill for 1 hour.

Pre-heat the oven to 180°C/350°F/Gas 4. Lightly grease a baking tray. On a lightly floured surface, roll out the dough to 3 mm (⅛ in) thick. Cut into 7.5 x 0.5-cm (3 x ¼-in) strips. Twist each strip and put them on the baking tray. Bake for about 6–8 minutes until golden brown.

Kedgeree

Notions of the old Empire are attached to this very classical dish and its origins as a breakfast dish are well forgotten as it now appears as the perfect light snack.

Serves 4

750 g (1½ lb) smoked haddock
600 ml (1 pint) milk
75 g (3 oz) butter
1 onion, finely chopped
250 ml (8 fl oz) basmati rice
(measured in a jug)

1 teaspoon curry powder (or more, if
you like it hot)
2 hard-boiled eggs, chopped
2 tablespoons chopped fresh parsley
Salt and freshly ground black pepper

Put the smoked haddock and milk in large frying pan. Bring to simmering point then simmer for 6–8 minutes until just tender. Drain off the milk and reserve. Using two forks, flake the fish into large pieces, cover and keep warm.

Melt 50 g (2 oz) of the butter in a pan, add the onion and cook for 5 minutes until soft. Add the rice and cook for a further minute. Sprinkle over the curry powder, stir and add the reserved milk. Bring to the boil, cover and cook gently, stirring occasionally, for about 15 minutes, until tender.

Add the fish, chopped eggs, parsley and the remaining 25 g (1 oz) of butter. Using a fork, gently mix the ingredients together. Check and, if necessary, season with salt and pepper.

Spiced Meat Loaf

❧⚜❧

I've always been a huge Meat Loaf fan, but more recently I've become intrigued by Take That! This is a dish which keeps well in the fridge and allows you to enjoy a slice whenever your fancy takes it.

Serves 8

450 g (1 lb) lean minced steak
225 g (8 oz) sausagemeat
   (Cumberland is good)
2 onions, minced
1 green pepper, seeded and finely
   chopped
1 red pepper, seeded and finely
   chopped
1 tablespoon tomato purée

2 garlic cloves, crushed
3 tablespoons chopped fresh parsley
1 tablespoon chopped fresh tarragon
50 g (2 oz) fresh white breadcrumbs
1 size 1 egg, beaten
Pinch of cayenne pepper
1 tablespoon Dijon mustard
Salt and freshly ground black pepper

Pre-heat the oven to 180°C/350°F/Gas 4.

Lightly grease a 1-kg (2-lb) loaf tin. Mix all the ingredients together and season with salt and pepper. Transfer the mixture to the prepared tin and cover with foil. Cook in the oven for 1½ hours. Remove from the oven and leave in the tin until cold and set.

Flan Forestière

❦

I love this served either hot or cold, although it has to be said that a plate
of this, chilled, with a selection of pickles takes a lot of beating.

Serves 4–6

FOR THE PASTRY:
100 g (4 oz) plain flour
Pinch of salt
25 g (1 oz) butter
25 g (1 oz) lard
1 egg yolk
2 tablespoons cold water

FOR THE FILLING:
150 ml (5 fl oz) milk
1 size 1 egg, beaten

1 tablespoon olive oil
50 g (2 oz) bacon, chopped
50 g (2 oz) onion, finely chopped
1 garlic clove, crushed
50 g (2 oz) mushrooms, the wilder
  the better!
1 tablespoon chopped fresh coriander
25 g (1 oz) Gruyère
Salt and freshly ground black pepper

To make the pastry, sift the flour and salt into a bowl. Rub in the butter and lard
until the mixture resembles breadcrumbs. Make a hollow in the centre, add the
egg yolk and water and mix together to form a dough. Chill for 1 hour.

Meanwhile, prepare the filling. Bring the milk to the boil and pour onto the
egg, mix together and season with salt and pepper to taste. Heat the oil in a
frying pan, add the bacon, onion and garlic and cook for 3–4 minutes until
softened. Add the mushrooms and cook for a further 2 minutes.

Pre-heat the oven to 180°C/350°F/Gas 4.

On a lightly floured surface, roll out the pastry and use to line an 18-cm
(7-in) flan ring. Add the bacon mixture then pour on the milk mixture. Sprinkle
the coriander and the cheese on top. Bake in the oven for 20–25 minutes until
firm to the touch.

A Warm Salad of Oatmeal Herrings

I recall thinking that I could hear the distant roll of bagpipes in the background whilst enjoying a plate of oatmeal herrings when filming in the Highlands (Skye to be precise). Then I realized it was merely my romantic fantasies playing havoc with my emotions. Lovely dish – even without the bagpipes.

Serves 4

4 herrings, cleaned, boned and
   heads and tails removed
100 g (4 oz) butter, melted
225 g (8 oz) fine oatmeal
Oil, for frying

Juice of 1 lemon
Salt and freshly ground black pepper
A selection of dressed salad leaves,
   to serve

Dip the herrings in melted butter, season with salt and pepper and then coat them in the oatmeal.

Heat a little oil in a frying pan. Place the fillets, flesh side down, into the pan and cook for 2–3 minutes on both sides until tender. Place onto plates with the dressed salad leaves. Add the lemon juice to the pan, mix together and spoon over the herrings. Serve warm.

Creamed Mushrooms on Garlic Toast

Perfect when all you fancy is a thrown-together dish that is easy to produce
yet delightful to eat.

Serves 4–6

750 g (1½ lb) mushrooms
150 g (6 oz) butter
50 g (2 oz) onion, finely chopped
1 tablespoon snipped fresh chives
1 tablespoon French mustard
175 ml (6 fl oz) white wine
Pinch of paprika

2 garlic cloves, crushed
1 tablespoon chopped fresh parsley
4–6 slices white bread
150 ml (5 fl oz) double cream
Juice of ½ a lemon
Salt and freshly ground black pepper

Slice the mushrooms. Heat 75 g (3 oz) of the butter in a pan and add the mushrooms. Add the onion and chives to the pan and cook for 3–5 minutes until tender. Add the mustard and white wine, and boil until reduced by half then add the paprika. Remove from the heat.

Beat the remaining 75 g (3 oz) of butter until soft then add the garlic and parsley and mix together. Toast the bread and spread with the garlic butter. Return the mushrooms to the heat and add the cream and lemon juice. Season with salt and pepper to taste and heat through. Serve on the toast.

Angels on Horseback

❦

Utter decadence is a plate of Angels on Horseback and a bottle of Krug, but, interestingly, they're just as nice, feet up in front of the telly with a glass of lager!

Serves 4

12 oysters
12 rashers streaky bacon, rinded
4 slices white bread

Butter, for spreading
Freshly ground black pepper

Remove the oysters from their shells, clean and season with pepper. Wrap a piece of bacon around each oyster and secure with a cocktail stick. Cook under a grill until the bacon is crisp on all sides.

Toast the slices of bread, butter them and cut into thirds. Place a bacon-wrapped oyster on each slice and serve immediately.

Devils on Horseback

❦

If you can accept that there are Angels on Horseback then you must accept Devils on Horseback! This is the naughty version.

Serves 4

12 cooked prunes, stoned
2 tablespoons chutney – whichever you fancy!
12 slices streaky bacon, rinded

4 slices white bread
Butter, for spreading
Freshly ground black pepper

Using a teaspoon, fill the cavity of the prunes with the chutney. Season with pepper.

Wrap a slice of bacon around each prune and secure with a cocktail stick. Cook under a grill until the bacon is crisp on all sides.

Toast the slices of bread, butter them and cut into thirds. Place a bacon-wrapped prune on each slice. Serve immediately.

Aubergine and Tuna Bake

Aubergine is without doubt one of the most versatile ingredients available as a light snack. It's perfect, but it does need additional flavour and tuna does the trick. A little salad makes this a real treat.

Serves 4

2 aubergines
2 tablespoons olive oil
100 g (4 oz) canned tuna, in brine
25 g (1 oz) butter
25 g (1 oz) plain flour

300 ml (10 fl oz) milk
4 tablespoons freshly grated
   Parmesan
2 tablespoons chopped fresh parsley
Salt and freshly ground black pepper

Pre-heat the oven to 180°C/350°F/Gas 4.

Cut the aubergines lengthways and brush the surface of the flesh with oil. Using a sharp knife, make incisions across the flesh. Bake in the oven for 15–20 minutes until the flesh is tender.

Drain and mash the tuna. Melt the butter in a saucepan, add the flour and mix together to form a roux. Cook gently, beating, for 2–3 minutes. Remove from the heat and gradually add the milk, stirring to form a smooth sauce. Bring slowly to the boil and continue to cook, stirring, until the sauce thickens. Season with salt and pepper to taste. Stir in the tuna.

When the aubergines are cooked, scoop out the flesh, reserving the shells. Chop the flesh and add to the tuna mixture, then place in the aubergine shells. Mix together the Parmesan and parsley. Sprinkle over the surface of the aubergines and bake in the oven for 10–12 minutes until golden brown.

Parmesan Biscuits

❦

These shortbread type biscuits make an ideal snack between meals and are really lovely served as an appetizer just before a meal.

Makes about 48

225 g (8 oz) plain flour
½ teaspoon salt
175 g (6 oz) butter, softened
2 egg yolks, lightly beaten
100 g (4 oz) freshly grated
    Parmesan

1 tablespoon chopped fresh flatleaf
    parsley
Pinch of cayenne pepper
1 egg, lightly beaten, for glazing

Sift together the flour and salt into a bowl. Beat the butter with a wooden spoon until light and fluffy. Beat in a little flour, followed by a little of the egg yolks. Continue to do this until all has been incorporated. Add the Parmesan, parsley and cayenne. Mix to a smooth dough. Chill for at least 4 hours.

Pre-heat the oven to 160°C/325°F/Gas 3.

On a lightly floured surface, roll out the dough to 5 mm (¼ in) thick. Using a 5-cm (2-in) plain round cutter, cut into rounds and place onto lightly greased baking trays. Glaze each biscuit with beaten egg and bake in the oven for 18–25 minutes until golden brown. Cool on a wire rack.

EGGS

Eggs must be one of the most versatile ingredients available and appear top of my league of essential foods to store at home. When all else fails and you haven't had time to shop, an omelette is always a life-saver. This is just one example of an egg dish that is willing to act as host to anything that may be lying in your fridge or storecupboard. You will find the range of recipes in this chapter are all of equal versatility.

There is often confusion over the difference between white and brown eggs, with the latter being healthier. The fact is they are identical. As for quality of eggs, I'm delighted we've returned to the good old days of date-stamping them.

Once purchased, they should be stored in a cool place. If this happens to be the fridge then do take them out at least two hours before needed so as to let them to at least begin to thaw out!

Plan the use of your eggs carefully. If a recipe calls for egg yolks, leave enough time during your cooking to make meringue shells out of its whites, and if the recipe requires whites, use the yolks to make a small bowl of fresh mayonnaise.

Egg in Cocotte with a Creamed Chicken Purée

This has to be the purest and simplest way to cook an egg. The chicken purée enhances the dish and you can adapt the recipe by using a vegetable purée such as spinach.

Serves 4

100 g (4 oz) cooked chicken breast, finely diced
75 ml (3 fl oz) double cream
1 tablespoon chopped fresh coriander

4 size 1 eggs
25 g (1 oz) butter, softened
Salt and freshly ground black pepper

Pre-heat the oven to 180°C/350°F/Gas 4.

Lightly butter 4 individual ramekin dishes. Mix together the chicken with half of the cream and the coriander. Season to taste with salt and pepper and place into the bottom of each dish.

Break an egg, without disturbing the yolk, on to the chicken purée. Season lightly with salt and pepper and spoon a little cream over each one. Add a knob of butter to the centre of each dish. Stand the dishes in a roasting tin then pour in enough hot water to come halfway up the sides of the dishes. Bake in the oven for 14–16 minutes until the eggs have set. Serve immediately.

Bubble and Squeak topped with a Fried Egg

❦

This recipe brings childhood memories flooding back. Over the past few years it has developed into an elegant dish, gracing the tables of many fine restaurants. What a great way to serve a fried egg. (It is particularly important in this recipe not to mix the metric and imperial weights.)

Serves 4

150 g (or 6 oz) butter
50 g (2 oz) bacon rashers, finely diced
1 tablespoon snipped fresh chives
1 garlic clove, crushed
75 g (3 oz) leeks, finely sliced
50 g (2 oz) cooked carrot, finely diced

100 g (4 oz) cooked green cabbage, finely chopped
Salt and freshly ground black pepper
350 g (12 oz) cooked potatoes, mashed
4 size 1 eggs
Oil, for shallow frying
Dressed salad leaves, to garnish

Melt 50 g (2 oz) of the butter in a pan then add the bacon, chives, garlic, leeks and carrot. Cook for 5 minutes without browning. Add the cabbage and season with salt and pepper. Mix this mixture into the mashed potato, check and adjust the seasoning if necessary. Divide the mixture into 4 equal pieces and shape each into a cake. Melt the remaining 100 g (4 oz) of butter in a large frying pan. Add the potato cakes and cook on both sides for about 5 minutes until golden brown. In a separate pan, fry the eggs in the oil. Place the potato cakes on 4 plates and top with a fried egg. Garnish with the dressed salad leaves.

Poached Egg on a bed of Creamed Spinach and Croûtons with an Ivory Sauce

❧❀❧

Egg and spinach is a traditional combination that works well together.
Be sure not to overcook the eggs and go gently with the seasoning in the sauce.
The delicate flavour of the egg and spinach should dominate and you need a
runny egg for that to happen.

Serves 4

450 g (1 lb) fresh spinach
3 slices of white bread, crusts removed
100 g (4 oz) butter
1 garlic clove, crushed
1 tablespoon chopped fresh coriander
4 size 1 eggs
2 tablespoons white wine vinegar
4 large coriander leaves, for garnish
Pinch of freshly grated nutmeg
Salt and freshly ground black pepper

FOR THE IVORY SAUCE:
40 g (1½ oz) butter
25 g (1 oz) leek, finely sliced
½ garlic clove, crushed
25 g (1 oz) plain flour
350 ml (12 fl oz) strong chicken stock
2 tablespoons meat extract
50 ml (2 fl oz) double cream
Juice of ½ a lemon

First make the sauce. Melt 40 g (1½ oz) butter in a pan, add the leek and garlic and cook for 2–3 minutes until soft. Add the flour and, stirring continuously, cook until it looks sandy in texture. Remove from the heat and gradually stir in the stock then add the meat extract. Bring slowly to the boil and continue to cook, stirring, until the sauce thickens. Cook gently for 1–2 minutes. Add the cream and season with salt, pepper and lemon juice. Cover the surface of the sauce with a sheet of greaseproof paper and keep warm.

Wash the spinach, discarding any large stalks, then cook with 2 tablespoons of water and a little salt for about 5 minutes until tender. Drain and squeeze out the excess moisture. Set aside. Cut the bread slices into small cubes. Melt 75 g (3 oz) butter in a large frying pan and add the cubed bread, garlic and coriander. Cook for 3–4 minutes until golden brown. Remove from the pan and set aside. Melt the remaining 25 g (1 oz) of butter in the frying pan, add the cooked spinach, grated nutmeg and salt and pepper to taste. When hot, pour a small quantity of the ivory sauce into the pan and mix thoroughly. The spinach should only be moistened with the sauce. Using a 7.5-cm (3-in) ring mould placed on to the centre of a plate, divide the spinach by packing it into the mould and repeat for the other 3 plates.

Poach the eggs in a large deep pan of boiling water with the vinegar and Pinch of salt for 3–5 minutes until lightly set.

Spoon the garlic croûtons over the spinach. Drain the poached eggs on a clean cloth, then place them on top of the croûtons. Pour over the sauce and garnish with coriander leaves.

Tortilla

This classic Spanish omelette is so underrated in this country. It tastes so good that it is well worth the little extra effort involved in making it. Serve with warm Spanish or Italian bread.

Serves 4

2 tablespoons olive oil
15 g (½ oz) butter
2 medium potatoes, thinly sliced
1 garlic clove, crushed
1 large onion, sliced
1 red pepper, seeded and chopped

1 green pepper, seeded and chopped
75 g (3 oz) continental sausage,
  finely diced
1 tablespoon chopped fresh parsley
4 size 1 eggs, lightly beaten
Salt and freshly ground black pepper

Heat the oil and butter in a large frying pan, add the potatoes and cook for 10–12 minutes, until softened and golden brown. Add the garlic and onion and cook for a further 2 minutes, then add the peppers, sausage and parsley and cook for 3–4 minutes.

Season the eggs with salt and pepper and pour over the cooked vegetables. Stir the eggs through the mixture to ensure that they are evenly distributed, then cook over a low heat for 8–10 minutes.

Once the bottom of the omelette has set, put a large plate over the pan, and holding pan and plate together, turn the pan upside down so that the omelette is transferred to the plate. Slide the omelette back into the pan and cook for a further 1–2 minutes until set underneath. Serve warm.

Egg and Parma Ham Croquettes

᭰᯼᭰

This also makes a delightful starter and is very easy to prepare. If you are unable to get Parma ham, or don't like the taste, then use bacon or cooked ham.

Serves 4

50 g (2 oz) butter
25 g (1 oz) plain flour
300 ml (10 fl oz) milk
6 hard-boiled eggs, diced
1 tablespoon snipped fresh chives
2 egg yolks
25 g (1 oz) Parma ham, finely diced

Plain flour, for dusting
1 egg, beaten
100 g (4 oz) fresh breadcrumbs
Oil, for deep frying
Salt and freshly ground black pepper
Tomato Sauce, to serve (page 63)

Melt 25 g (1 oz) butter in a pan. Add the flour and cook gently for 2 minutes, stirring. Remove from the heat and gradually stir in the milk to form a smooth sauce. Bring slowly to the boil and continue to cook, stirring, until the sauce thickens. Season with salt and pepper to taste.

Melt the remaining butter in a separate pan, then add the diced egg and chives. Stir in the white sauce, then add the egg yolks. Remove from the heat, add the Parma ham and mix together.

Spread the mixture onto a buttered baking tray, cover and chill for 2–3 hours. Divide the mixture into 4 or 8 equal pieces and with lightly floured hands, mould into croquettes. Roll each croquette in flour, then egg and finally coat in breadcrumbs. Heat the oil in a deep-fat fryer to 180°C/350°F. Place a few croquettes at a time into the oil and fry for 2–3 minutes until golden brown. Drain on kitchen paper and serve with Tomato Sauce.

Poached Egg with Griddled Aubergine and Creamed Curry Sauce

This makes a superb snack or starter. The eggs can be poached in advance and kept in a bowl of cold water for 2–3 hours. Reheat the eggs in a pan of hot water for a few seconds before serving.

Serves 4

1 large aubergine, sliced into 4 thick rounds
50 g (2 oz) butter
50 g (2 oz) shallots, finely chopped
½ garlic clove, crushed
2 large plump tomatoes, seeded and finely diced
1 tablespoon chopped fresh basil

1 tablespoon curry powder
2 tablespoons white wine
300 ml (10 fl oz) double cream
4 eggs
2 tablespoons white wine vinegar
Salt and freshly ground black pepper
Coriander leaves, to garnish

Sprinkle the aubergine with salt, place in a colander with a heavy object on top and leave for 15 minutes.

Melt 25 g (1 oz) of the butter in a pan. Add 25 g (1 oz) of the shallots and garlic and cook gently for 2 minutes without colouring. Add the diced tomatoes and basil. Season lightly with salt and pepper then set aside. Melt the remaining 25 g (1 oz) butter, add the remaining 25 g (1 oz) shallots and cook for 1 minute. Stir in the curry powder. Pour in the wine and boil until it has reduced by half. Add the cream, lower the heat and simmer until the sauce is thick enough to coat the back of a wooden spoon.

Poach the eggs in a large deep pan of boiling water with the vinegar and Pinch of salt for 3–5 minutes until lightly set. Rinse and dry the aubergines then cook on a hot griddle or in a grooved frying pan until browned. Place each aubergine slice on the centre of a plate. Cover with the tomato mixture and put a poached egg gently on top. Pour over the sauce and garnish with coriander leaves.

Buck Rarebit with Tomatoes and a Poached Egg

This adaptation of the old classic Welsh rarebit is, in my opinion, far nicer and much more interesting to eat.

Serves 4

15 g (½ oz) butter
15 g (½ oz) plain flour
175 ml (6 fl oz) milk
½ teaspoon English mustard
Pinch of cayenne pepper
2 teaspoons Worcestershire sauce
1 egg yolk
50 g (2 oz) Cheddar, grated

1 teaspoon chopped fresh parsley
4 eggs
1 tablespoon white wine vinegar
4 slices bread
Butter, for spreading
2 tomatoes, skinned and sliced
Salt and freshly ground black pepper

Melt the butter in a pan. Add the flour and cook for 1 minute, stirring. Remove from the heat and gradually stir in the milk. Bring slowly to the boil, and continue to cook, stirring, until the sauce thickens. Add the mustard, cayenne pepper and Worcestershire sauce.

Remove from the heat and add the egg yolk, cheese and parsley. Season to taste with salt and pepper.

Poach the eggs in a large deep pan of boiling water with the vinegar and a pinch of salt until lightly set. Toast the bread slices and spread with butter. Arrange the sliced tomatoes over the hot buttered toast, place a poached egg on top then cover with the rarebit mixture. Cook under a hot grill until golden brown.

Scotch Eggs

———————— ❧❦❧ ————————

A freshly made Scotch egg served warm with a crisp salad is pure joy.
The shopper who cooked this with me had been buying prepared Scotch eggs
for years and hadn't realized just how easy it is to make them fresh.
It's a good idea to experiment with different types of sausagemeat – makes it
much more fun!

Serves 4

450 g (1 lb) sausagemeat
4 hard-boiled eggs
75 g (3 oz) plain flour
1 egg, beaten

225 g (8 oz) fresh breadcrumbs
Oil, for deep frying
Tomato Sauce, to serve (page 63)

Divide the sausagemeat into 4 equal pieces. Dip each egg in the flour, shake off excess and wrap the meat around the eggs, moulding the meat so that it is an even thickness.

Dip the covered eggs in the flour, then in the beaten egg and finally into the breadcrumbs. Heat the oil in a deep-fat fryer to 160°C/325°F. Place the eggs in the oil and fry for 7–8 minutes until golden brown. Drain on kitchen paper and serve with Tomato Sauce (page 63).

Cheese and Spring Onion Soufflé

❧❀❧

The difference that spring onion makes to a standard cheese soufflé
is remarkable. Serve with a tomato and basil salad.

Serves 4

75 g (3 oz) butter
*50 g (2 oz) Parmesan, freshly
  grated*
*75 g (3 oz) spring onions, finely
  chopped*
2 tablespoons plain flour

150 ml (¼ pint) milk
Pinch of cayenne pepper
1 teaspoon Dijon mustard
100 g (4 oz) Cheddar, grated
3 size 1 eggs, separated
Salt and freshly ground black pepper

Pre-heat the oven to 190°C/375°F/Gas 5.

Melt 50 g (2 oz) of the butter and use to coat the base and sides of a 900-ml
(1½-pint) soufflé dish. Dust with the Parmesan. Melt the remaining butter in a
pan, add the spring onions and cook for 1 minute. Add the flour and mix to
form a roux. Cook gently for 2 minutes, stirring. Remove from the heat and
gradually stir in the milk, to produce a smooth sauce. Slowly bring to the boil
and continue to cook, stirring, until the sauce thickens. Season with cayenne
pepper and Dijon mustard and allow to cool slightly before adding the grated
cheese. Mix well together, then add the egg yolks.

Whisk the egg whites until they form stiff peaks. Add a third of the whites to
the sauce and beat together, then carefully fold in the remaining egg whites.

Spoon the soufflé mixture into the prepared dish and bake for 30–35 minutes
until well-risen and golden brown. Serve immediately.

Smoked Haddock Omelette with a Gruyère and Chive Sauce

This is real comfort food and, coupled with ease of preparation, it makes it the perfect dish for those moments when time is at a premium or you are feeling at your lowest. Do be sure to select real smoked haddock. The bright, heavily dyed variety should be avoided at all costs. If smoked haddock isn't available then any smoked fish, particularly smoked salmon, would suffice.

Serves 1

3 eggs
25 g (1 oz) butter
50 g (2 oz) smoked haddock, flaked
85 (3 fl oz) double cream

25 g (1 oz) Gruyère, grated
1 tablespoon snipped fresh chives
Salt and freshly ground black pepper

Beat the eggs in a bowl and season with salt and pepper. Heat the butter in a non-stick omelette pan, pour in the eggs and cook, drawing the eggs from the edges to the centre until set and golden underneath. Add the smoked haddock, then, using a palette knife, fold over a third of the omelette to the centre, then fold over the opposite third. Turn out onto a warmed flameproof serving dish, cover and keep warm.

Pour the cream into the hot pan and boil until reduced to one-third. Add the cheese, chives and salt and pepper to taste. Pour the sauce over the omelette and cook briefly under a hot grill to glaze the top. Serve immediately.

Egg, Bacon and Leek Flan

This is lovely whether it's served hot, warm or cold. You could substitute
225 g (8 oz) onions for the leeks, if wished.

Serves 4

100 g (4 oz) plain flour
Pinch of salt
50 g (2 oz) lard
1 tablespoon chopped fresh parsley
25 g (1 oz) butter
450 g (1 lb) leeks, finely chopped
100 g (4 oz) smoked bacon, finely
  diced

1 garlic clove, crushed
250 ml (10 fl oz) double cream
2 size 1 eggs
Pinch of freshly grated nutmeg
Salt and freshly ground black pepper

Sift the flour and salt into a large bowl. Add the lard and rub in as gently as possible until the mixture resembles sand. Add the parsley and 1–2 tablespoons of
cold water to form the pastry. Wrap in foil and chill for 2 hours.

Pre-heat the oven 180°C/350°F/Gas 4.

Roll out the pastry on a lightly floured surface and use to line a 20-cm (8-in)
flan tin. Prick the base and line with foil. Bake for 20–25 minutes until set.

Meanwhile, prepare the filling. Melt the butter in a pan, add the leeks, bacon
and garlic and cook gently for 5 minutes. Season with salt and pepper. Transfer
the mixture to the flan case, discarding the liquid.

In a pan gently warm the cream. Beat the eggs and mix in the cream. Season
with salt, pepper and nutmeg. Pour over the leeks and return to the oven for a
further 30–35 minutes until set.

Cheese-glazed Eggs filled with Wild Mushrooms

❦

This is a great starter and lends itself to being prepared in advance.
Any wild mushrooms can be used in this recipe and don't be afraid to
vary the cheese – use whichever is your favourite.

Serves 4

4 hard-boiled eggs
75 g (3 oz) butter
75 g (3 oz) shallots, finely chopped
150 g (8 oz) wild mushrooms, finely
  chopped
1 garlic clove, crushed
1 tablespoon chopped fresh parsley

25 g (1 oz) fresh white breadcrumbs
Pinch of cayenne pepper
25 g (1 oz) plain flour
300 ml (10 fl oz) milk
100 g (4 oz) Gruyère, grated
Salt and freshly ground black pepper

Cut the eggs in half lengthways, remove and sieve the yolk. Reserve the whites
for later. Melt 50 g (2 oz) of the butter in a pan, add the shallots, mushrooms
and garlic. Cook for 2 minutes, then add the parsley, breadcrumbs and sieved
egg yolks. Season with cayenne, salt and pepper. Cover and keep warm.

Melt the remaining 25 g (1 oz) butter in a pan, add the flour, mix to form a
roux and cook gently for 1 minute, stirring. Remove from the heat and gradually stir in the milk to form a smooth sauce. Bring slowly to the boil and cook,
stirring, until the sauce thickens. Add half of the grated cheese. Season with salt
and pepper to taste.

Fill the reserved egg whites with the mushroom mixture and place them on a
flameproof dish. Coat each half with the cheese sauce and cover with the
remaining grated cheese. Cook under a hot grill until brown.

PASTA, GNOCCHI AND RICE

The supermarkets these days stock a fabulous range of fresh pasta which must be the answer to a reluctant cook's prayer. It has to be the easiest ingredient in the world to deal with. A pan of boiling salted water and a watchful eye ensures that this simple ingredient is cooked in no time at all. Add to that a few other ingredients and just a touch of imagination, and a feast unfolds. Yet for all the ease of being able to purchase ready-made fresh pasta, I still prefer, when I have the time, to make it from scratch.

Pasta is simply a dough which is rolled out very thinly, usually with the use of a pasta machine (available at all good stores), then cut or shaped into specific-sized pieces. It really is a simple process which requires very little effort for huge rewards. It is a good idea to make a batch for the week and refrigerate the excess until needed, thus making life sweet and simple.

Once you've mastered the basic recipe, an egg pasta, then you can become really adventurous and add spinach, sun-dried tomatoes, finely diced black olives... the list is endless.

The term gnocchi simply means dumpling and you'll see from the recipes in this chapter that they are a most economical way to feed a family.

Rice forms part of a staple diet for many households and is always a handy storecupboard ingredient to accompany main dishes or to have for dessert. It's sensible to use the appropriate rice for your dish.

Patna – a long-grain rice most widely used for savoury dishes. It is grown in all parts of the world and the quality can vary enormously. I'm not particularly a fan of this type.

Basmati – an Indian rice, with great flavour and good for savoury dishes as it retains its individual quality.

Arborio – the best rice for a risotto I find. It has a fabulous flavour and is very starchy. Grown in Northern Italy and like a true Italian, it has lots of style.

Carolina – a generic term for short-grain rice, excellent for puddings.

Tortelloni in a Tuna and Lemon Dressing

Tuna and pasta is a lovely combination and it works particularly well in this recipe, due to the fact that tortelloni gathers the flavours so readily. Be sure not to overcook the pasta and also to drain it really well. Any excess moisture will weaken the flavour.

Serves 4

225 g (8 oz) tortelloni
75 g (3 oz) butter
50 g (2 oz) shallots, chopped
1 garlic clove, crushed
100 g (4 oz) cooked tuna, mashed
1 tablespoon chopped fresh parsley
½ tablespoon chopped fresh dill
Grated rind and juice of 1 lemon

175 ml (6 fl oz) dry white wine
½ teaspoon paprika
300 ml (10 fl oz) cream
Salt and freshly ground black pepper
1 tablespoon chopped fresh dill, to
  garnish
Freshly grated Parmesan, to serve

Cook the pasta in a large pan of boiling salted water for about 15 minutes until just tender. Drain and refresh under cold running water. Drain again and set aside.

Melt 50 g (2 oz) of the butter in a pan, add the shallots and garlic, and cook for 1 minute without browning. Add the tuna and herbs, mix well and pour in the lemon rind, juice and white wine. Boil until reduced by half then add the paprika and cream. Bring to the boil and season with salt and pepper. Keep the sauce warm.

Melt the remaining 25 g (1 oz) butter in a wide pan, add the drained pasta, season lightly to taste, and reheat. Pour the tuna and lemon dressing over the pasta, mix well and transfer to a serving dish. Garnish with the chopped dill. Serve the Parmesan separately.

Penne with an Egg and Bacon Sauce

This is a very substantial pasta dish which packs in taste along with substance. The penne can be cooked in advance if required. Simply drain and wash it under cold running water and then reheat it by either placing it in a pan of hot salted water or tossing it in a little hot butter. Be sure to season it through because it can lose much of its seasoning during washing.

Serves 4

350 g (12 oz) penne
600 ml (1 pint) milk
75 g (3 oz) butter
50 g (2 oz) onion, chopped
50 g (2 oz) bacon, diced
1 tablespoon chopped fresh parsley
40 g (1½ oz) plain flour

3 hard-boiled eggs, chopped
75 ml (3 fl oz) double cream
3 tomatoes, sliced
50 g (2 oz) Parmesan, freshly grated
Salt and freshly ground black pepper

Cook the penne in a large pan of boiling salted water for 10 minutes until just tender. Drain and refresh under cold running water. Leave in the colander or sieve until required.

Pre-heat the oven to 230°C/450°F/Gas 8.

Bring the milk to the boil then set aside.

Heat the butter in a pan, add the onion, bacon and parsley. Cook for 1 minute, then add the flour and stir together to form a roux. Remove from the heat and gradually whisk in the milk to form a smooth sauce. Bring slowly to the boil and continue to cook, stirring, until the sauce thickens. Add the chopped eggs, cream and season with salt and pepper to taste. Tip the penne into the sauce and mix thoroughly. Transfer to an ovenproof dish and cover the top with the sliced tomatoes. Sprinkle with the Parmesan and bake for 10 minutes until golden brown.

Fresh Cannelloni with a Spinach and Feta Cheese Filling

One of the delightful things about pasta dishes is the simplicity involved in its preparation. For very little effort, the gastronomic rewards are high. I have fond memories of the look of sheer horror on the face of the victim caught with a packet of cannelloni when told that he was about to be confronted with the task of making fresh cannelloni. I left his house knowing that he was converted.

Serves 4

225 g (8 oz) plain flour
¼ teaspoon salt
40 ml (1½ fl oz) oil
100 ml (3½ fl oz) water
50 g (2 oz) shallots, finely chopped
1 garlic clove, crushed
1 tablespoon chopped fresh coriander
275 g (10 oz) spinach, chopped

100 g (4 oz) feta cheese, diced
Freshly grated nutmeg
600 ml (1 pint) chicken or vegetable
  stock
4 tablespoons Madeira or sherry
1 tablespoon arrowroot
Salt and freshly ground black pepper

Sift the flour and salt into a bowl. Make a hollow in the centre, add the oil and water and mix to form a smooth dough. Cover and leave the dough to rest for 30 minutes.

Mix together the shallots, garlic, coriander, spinach and feta cheese. Season with salt and pepper and a little grated nutmeg.

On a lightly floured surface, roll out the dough as thinly as possible. Cut into 6 x 6-cm (3 x 3-in) squares. Cook the dough squares in boiling salted water for 15–18 minutes until tender. Drain and pat dry.

Place the spinach mixture onto the cannelloni and roll up. Transfer to a lightly buttered ovenproof dish and cover to keep moist.

Pre-heat the oven to 180°C/350°F/Gas 4.

Bring the stock to the boil, then add the Madeira or sherry. Moisten the arrowroot with a little cold water to form a smooth paste and whisk it into the boiling liquid. Pour the sauce over the cannelloni. Bake for 10 minutes until golden brown.

Fresh Noodles with Nut Brown Butter and Shredded Mushrooms

❧

I caught a shopper in whose trolley I spied a packet of dried noodles. After a little teasing and some smooth talking, I managed to persuade her to let me and the crew invade the privacy of her kitchen in order to show her just how simple it is to make them fresh. Not only are freshly made noodles nicer to eat than their dried counterparts, but I find them therapeutic to handle.

Serves 4

225 g (8 oz) plain flour
¼ teaspoon salt
1 egg
1 dessertspoon olive oil
4 egg yolks
25 ml (1 fl oz) milk

FOR THE BUTTER SAUCE:
75 g (3 oz) butter
1 tablespoon snipped fresh chives
¼ garlic clove, crushed
75 g (3 oz) cep or girolle mushrooms, finely shredded
Salt and freshly ground black pepper

Sift the flour and salt into a bowl. Make a hollow in the centre and add the remaining pasta ingredients and mix to form a smooth dough. Cover and chill for 30 minutes.

Cut the dough in half. On a lightly floured surface, roll out each piece of dough to a rectangle measuring 7.5 x 30 cm (3 x 10 in). Cover with a clean tea-towel and leave to rest for 3 hours.

Cut the dough into 3-mm (⅛-in) wide strips. Cook the noodles in plenty of boiling salted water for 14–15 minutes until tender. Drain, refresh under cold running water then drain again.

Heat the butter in a wide pan, add the chives, garlic and mushrooms and cook over a fierce heat. Once the butter begins to turn brown reduce the heat and add the noodles. Toss them gently, ensuring that they retain their shape. Season with salt and pepper to taste and serve hot.

Rustic Bolognese

❧✿❧

This authentic Italian dish is quite different from the more commonly known recipe. It is beautifully moist and accompanies pasta well. Serve with a bowl of freshly cooked spaghetti.

Serves 4

2 tablespoons olive oil
50 g (2 oz) onion, chopped
2 garlic cloves, crushed
50 g (2 oz) celery, chopped
50 g (2 oz) leek, sliced
50 g (2 oz) carrot, chopped
175 g (6 oz) coarsely minced pork

50 g (2 oz) pork fat, finely chopped
3 tablespoons tomato purée
300 ml (½ pint) hot chicken stock
475 ml (16 fl oz) white wine
1 bouquet garni
Salt and freshly ground black pepper

Heat the oil in a pan, add the onion and garlic and cook for 1 minute. Add the celery, leek and carrot, mix well and add the minced pork. Cook gently for 2 minutes. Add the pork fat and cook for a further 2 minutes.

Mix the tomato purée with the chicken stock and wine and add to the bolognese. Season with salt and pepper and add the bouquet garni. Cover with a lid and simmer gently for 20 minutes. Remove the lid and cook for a further 10 minutes to reduce the cooking liquid.

Remove the bouquet garni, check and adjust the seasoning if necessary. Serve hot with spaghetti.

Gnocchi Romaine

This dish was demonstrated following the purchase of semolina by two students from Canterbury who had a liking for baked beans straight from the tin and semolina pudding to follow. The idea was to show the versatility of this ingredient and get them away from the baked beans!

Serves 4

600 ml (1 pint) milk
100 g (4 oz) semolina
Freshly ground nutmeg
1 egg yolk
75 g (3 oz) Parmesan, freshly grated
50 g (2 oz) butter
1 tablespoon olive oil
50 g (2 oz) onion, chopped
1 garlic clove, chopped

450 g (1 lb) tomatoes, skinned, seeded and chopped
1 tablespoon tomato purée
150 ml (5 fl oz) chicken or vegetable stock
175 ml (6 fl oz) white wine
Salt and freshly ground black pepper
Chopped fresh parsley, to garnish

Bring the milk to the boil. Using a whisk, add the semolina. Season with salt, pepper and a little nutmeg. Cook gently for 5–8 minutes until really thick, stirring to prevent it from sticking to the pan. Remove from the heat. Cool slightly then add the egg yolk and 25 g (1 oz) of the Parmesan. Spread the mixture evenly in a buttered tray to a thickness of 1 cm (½ in). Melt 25 g (1 oz) of the butter and pour over the top. Leave to cool.

Meanwhile, prepare the sauce. Heat the oil in a pan, add the onion and garlic and cook for 2 minutes without browning. Add the tomatoes and tomato purée. Mix well and pour in the stock and white wine. Bring to the boil and season with salt and pepper. Simmer very gently for 10 minutes. Cover and keep warm.

Pre-heat the oven to 230°C/450°F/Gas 8.

Using a 5-cm (2-in) round cutter, cut out the gnocchi. Place the excess gnocchi into the centre of a buttered ovenproof dish and arrange the gnocchi rounds neatly on top. Dust with the remaining 50 g (2 oz) Parmesan and dot with the remaining 25 g (1 oz) of butter. Bake in the oven for 10–15 minutes until golden brown. Pour the sauce around the edge of the gnocchi and serve sprinkled with the chopped parsley.

Gnocchi Florentine

— ❧❀❧ —

The key to this recipe lies in planning ahead. Bake enough potatoes to accompany a meal for one day and for this recipe to be served the following day. If you have difficulty obtaining, or you dislike Parma ham, you could use a little cooked bacon or plain boiled ham, although it must be said that the flavour from Parma ham really adds to the dish.

Serves 4

450 g (1 lb) large potatoes
1 egg yolk
225 g (8 oz) fresh spinach
50 g (2 oz) Parma ham, finely chopped

25 g (1 oz) Parmesan, freshly grated
15 g (½ oz) plain flour
75 g (3 oz) butter
2 tablespoons snipped fresh chives
Salt and freshly ground black pepper

Pre-heat the oven to 200°C/400°F/Gas 6.

Scrub and prick the potatoes and bake for 1–1½ hours until tender. Cut in half, scoop out the flesh and mash. Season with salt and pepper, add the egg yolk and mix well together. Cook the spinach, in only the water clinging to the leaves after washing, for 5–10 minutes until tender. Drain well, pressing out any excess water, and chop finely. Add to the potato gnocchi along with the Parma ham and Parmesan.

Add the flour and mix together, adding a little more if necessary, so that the mixture can be rolled. With floured hands, shape into small balls. Cook the gnocchi in plenty of boiling salted water for 5–10 minutes until they rise to the top of the pan. Drain in a colander.

Heat the butter in a frying pan and reheat the gnocchi. Add the chives just before serving.

Paris-style Gnocchi

This inexpensive, easy-to-make gnocchi really does provide an economical filling meal. You might recognize the main components of the dish as the basis for choux pastry, and you would be correct.

Serves 4

FOR THE GNOCCHI:
50 g (2 oz) butter
120 ml (4 fl oz) water
65 g (2½ oz) plain flour
2 eggs, beaten

FOR THE SAUCE:
300 ml (10 fl oz) milk
40 g (1½ oz) butter

40 g (1½ oz) plain flour
50 g (2 oz) Gruyère, grated
Pinch of cayenne pepper
Salt and freshly ground black pepper

TO FINISH:
50 g (2 oz) butter
25 g (1 oz) Parmesan, freshly grated

To make the gnocchi put the butter and water in a pan and heat gently until the butter has melted, then bring to the boil. Remove from the heat. Tip all the flour at once into the hot liquid and, using a wooden spoon, mix to a smooth paste. Allow to cool then beat in the eggs, a little at a time.

Transfer the mixture to a piping bag filled with a large plain tube. Bring a large pan of salted water to the boil then simmer. Pipe small pieces, the size of a thumbnail, into the simmering water. Cook gently for 10 minutes, drain and set aside.

To make the sauce, bring the milk to the boil then set aside. Melt 40 g (1½ oz) butter in a pan, add the remaining 40 g (1½ oz) flour, and cook for 1 minute, stirring. Remove from the heat and gradually stir in the milk. Bring slowly to the boil and continue to cook, stirring, until the sauce thickens. Remove from the heat and beat in the cheese. Season with the cayenne, salt and pepper.

Heat the remaining 50 g (2 oz) butter in a shallow pan and gently fry the gnocchi for 5 minutes. Transfer the gnocchi to a flameproof serving dish, cover with the cheese sauce and sprinkle with Parmesan. Cook under a hot grill until brown. Serve hot.

Spaghetti in a Tomato and Basil Sauce

❧❧❧

This is a perfect dish for those whose tastes are relatively plain and prefer their pasta tasty but simple. The sauce can be used to accompany any dish – fish, meat or poultry.

Serves 4

FOR THE TOMATO SAUCE:
2 tablespoons olive oil
75 g (3 oz) onions, finely chopped
2 garlic cloves, crushed
1 tablespoon chopped fresh basil
400-g (14-oz) can chopped tomatoes
2 tablespoons tomato purée
120 ml (4 fl oz) white wine

Pinch of sugar
Dash of Worcestershire sauce
2 drops Tabasco sauce
Salt and freshly ground black pepper

FOR THE PASTA:
350 g (12 oz) spaghetti
50 g (2 oz) butter

To prepare the sauce, heat the oil in a pan, add the onions and garlic and fry for about 5 minutes until softened but not browned. Add the basil and chopped tomatoes and cook gently for 2–3 minutes, then add the tomato purée and white wine. Cook for a further 5 minutes, then add the sugar, Worcestershire and Tabasco sauce, and season with salt and pepper. Reduce the heat and simmer gently for 10 minutes.

Meanwhile, cook the spaghetti in a large pan of boiling salted water for about 10 minutes until just tender.

Melt the butter in a pan. Drain the pasta, add to the butter and season with salt and pepper. Add the tomato sauce, mix together and serve.

Risotto with Prosciutto and Tomato

—— ❧❧❧ ——

The combination of prosciutto with the garlic and tomatoes in this dish smacks of Italian sunshine. If you have difficulty getting prosciutto then simply use any cured ham.

Serves 4

50 ml (2 fl oz) olive oil
150 g (5 oz) onions, finely chopped
750 g (1½ lb) ripe tomatoes,
* skinned, seeded and chopped*
225 g (8 oz) arborio rice
1 garlic clove, crushed
550 ml (18 fl oz) hot chicken stock

Pinch of saffron
25 g (1 oz) butter
75 g (3 oz) Parmesan, freshly grated
50 g (2 oz) prosciutto, finely chopped
Salt and freshly ground black pepper
2 tablespoons chopped fresh basil

Heat 25 ml (1 fl oz) olive oil in a pan, add the onions and cook for 1 minute without browning. Stir in the tomatoes and simmer for 10 minutes.

Heat the remaining oil in a separate pan and add the rice and garlic. Stir to prevent this from sticking to the pan, then add the cooked tomato and hot stock. Mix in the saffron. Season with salt and pepper.

Cover the pan and simmer for 20 minutes until the rice is tender and all the stock has been absorbed. Using a fork, stir in the butter, Parmesan and prosciutto. Serve garnished with the basil.

RIGHT: *Bubble and Squeak topped with a Fried Egg*
OVERLEAF: *Devilled Chicken Livers* on a timbale of *Rice Pilaff,*
and *Mussels in a Light Saffron Broth*
PAGES 68–72: *Lamb Cutlets baked with a Rice and Onion Crust*
and *Roast Sea Bass with Herb-crumbed Garlic and a Rich Wine and Mushroom Sauce;*
Braised Breasts of Barbary Duckling served with Roasted Shallots and Garlic
and *Fillet of Beef with Wild Mushrooms and Mango;*
Stuffed Loin of Pork on a bed of Lentils with Caramelized Apples

Rice Pilaff

❧❀❧

The lovely thing about this rice dish is that you can play around with it. Rice pilaff acts as a great host dish to other ingredients so if, for example, you fancy a few pine kernels, green peppers or chillies, then simply add them!

Serves 4

750 ml (1¼ pints) chicken stock
75 g (3 oz) butter
75 g (3 oz) onions, finely diced
1 garlic clove, crushed

225 g (8 oz) long-grain rice
Salt and freshly ground black pepper
75 g (3 oz) Gruyère, grated, to serve

Heat the chicken stock in a pan. Melt 50 g (2 oz) of the butter in a pan then add the onions and garlic and cook for 2 minutes, without browning, until soft. Add the rice and mix together. Ladle in sufficient stock just to cover the rice, season with salt and then simmer gently for 5 minutes until all the liquid has been absorbed.

Gradually add the remaining stock over a period of 5 minutes. Once all the stock has been absorbed and the rice is tender, adjust the seasoning with salt and pepper. Add the remaining 25 g (1 oz) of butter and, using a fork, mix through. Serve the grated cheese separately.

FISH AND SHELLFISH

The test of a good cook is never better judged than by how well he or she has cooked the fish.

As a cook I consider fish and shellfish to be the most enjoyable to prepare. They both require very little preparation and cooking and, indeed, the simpler the recipe is the better the result.

When selecting fish, try to remember these simple guidelines. The longer the fish is out of water, the drier it becomes. There should be a sea slime to the fish which should smell fresh and not ammoniac. The eyes should be full and bright, scales should lie flat and should not be dry or broken. There should also be a deep red colour behind the gills and the flesh should be springy.

The rules for choosing shellfish are even simpler: buy it alive or, if you can't face the awful task of you know what!, buy it from a reputable supplier and assume that it needs to be eaten the same day. Shellfish, once past its sell-by date, can make you very ill. Take no chances.

Purchasing any form of food is a skill in its own right but with fresh fish or shellfish, it is particularly important as deterioration happens so quickly. Fish and shellfish must be stored in a refrigerator right up until required and then cooked and served immediately.

I always buy my fish on the bone – it's cheaper and the bones can be used to make fish stock. Simply chop the bones (minus the head) of flat white fish such as plaice or sole, and cook in a little clarified butter with chopped onions, leeks, a little garlic and fresh herbs for 3–4 minutes. Top up with water, lemon juice and a little wine and gently simmer for 20 minutes. Once it's cooked, strain and cool and use as required.

Salmon Steak baked in Paper with a Spaghetti of Cucumber

Reputedly, cooking en papillote has the effect of retaining all of the flavour of the salmon and I'm quite sure that this is the case. Serve them simply with boiled new potatoes.

Serves 4

1 small cucumber
A little butter, for greasing
Juice of 1½ lemons
4 salmon steaks, 175 g (6 oz) each
4 sprigs plus 1 teaspoon chopped fresh dill
175 ml (6 fl oz) white wine

2 tablespoons water
2 tablespoons white wine vinegar
25 g (1 oz) shallots, finely chopped
300 ml (10 fl oz) double cream
100 g (4 oz) unsalted butter
Salt and freshly ground black pepper

Pre-heat the oven to 180°C/350°F/Gas 4.

Peel and thinly slice the cucumber lengthways, then cut each length into spaghetti-like strips.

Lightly butter 4 large pieces of foil and place the cucumber on the centre of each. Add the juice of 1 lemon and season with salt and pepper. Place the salmon steaks on top, season with salt and pepper and place a sprig of dill on each. Bring the sides of foil up to form a little parcel. Pour in the wine and seal the edges of the foil together. Bake in the oven for 30 minutes.

Put the water, wine vinegar and shallots in a pan and boil until reduced by two-thirds. Leave to cool slightly. Add the cream and gradually whisk in two-thirds of the butter, a little at a time. Return the sauce to a very low heat, whisk harder and add the remaining butter. Season with the remaining lemon juice and the chopped dill.

Using a fish slice, remove the salmon and cucumber intact from the parcels, drain well and sit them in the centre of a serving plate. Serve hot.

A Mousse of Salmon served on a Lemon and Fennel Dressing

⸻ ❦ ⸻

Salmon lends itself perfectly to being used for a mousse. Its meaty texture is broken down, allowing the full flavour to dominate.

Serves 4

225 g (8 oz) fresh salmon, skinned and boned
1 egg white
375 ml (13 fl oz) double cream
2 tablespoons snipped fresh chives
Pinch of paprika
2 leeks
Butter, for greasing
175 ml (6 fl oz) dry white wine
120 ml (4 fl oz) dry vermouth

25 g (1 oz) shallots, finely chopped
2 tablespoons chopped fresh fennel
1 bay leaf
175 g (6 oz) unsalted butter, cubed and chilled
Juice of 1 lemon
Salt and white pepper
100 g (4 oz) tomato flesh, diced, to garnish
12 sprigs of fennel leaves, to garnish

Blend the salmon to a fine purée in a food processor. Add the egg white and mix together. Push the mixture through a fine sieve. Lightly whip 300 ml (10 fl oz) of the cream then fold into the salmon mixture. Add the chives and season with paprika, salt and pepper. Place into a fridge to chill.

Trim roots and dark tough ends of the leeks. Cut them in half widthways, then into rectangular strips measuring 13 x 1 cm (5 x ½ in). Blanch them for 1 minute in a pan of boiling salted water. Refresh under cold water, drain and pat dry. Butter 4 ramekin dishes. Select the best leeks and use to line the dishes, from the centre, up the sides, ensuring that there is sufficient overhang to cover the top of the moulds. Ideally alternate between green and white leaves. Fill each ramekin with the salmon mousse and fold over the excess leek. Cover with cling film, place in a pan of gently simmering water, to come halfway up the sides of the dishes, and cover with a lid. Cook for 12–15 minutes until set.

Meanwhile, prepare the sauce. Put the wine, vermouth, shallots, chopped fennel and bay leaf in a pan, and boil until reduced to one-third. Add the remaining 75 ml (3 fl oz) of cream and reduce the heat. Gradually whisk in the butter, a little at a time. Add the lemon juice and season with salt and pepper.

Strain the sauce into a serving jug. Carefully turn out the mousses onto warmed plates and pat dry any excess liquid. Pour the sauce around the mousses and garnish with 3 little mounds of the tomato flesh around the outside of each mousse. Serve garnished with a small fennel leaf on the tomatoes.

Lobster Thermidor

Everybody, at least once in their lifetime, should taste lobster. It has a unique ability to be able to take on the flavours of added ingredients yet retain its own distinct flavour. Its texture makes other shellfish seem boring.
A good fishmonger will prepare the lobster for you and if you wander around supermarkets long enough there's even a chance you'll find me and I'll cook it for you! Serve with a basket of chips – yes, chips!

Serves 2

1 cooked lobster, about 550 g (1¼ lb) in weight, halved, flesh removed and the shell cleaned
50 g (2 oz) butter
50 g (2 oz) shallots, finely chopped
1 garlic clove, crushed
1 tablespoon chopped fresh parsley
1 teaspoon French mustard

175 ml (6 fl oz) white wine
3 tablespoons brandy
150 ml (5 fl oz) plus 2 tablespoons double cream
Juice of ½ a lemon
15 g (½ oz) Parmesan, grated
1 egg yolk
Salt and freshly ground black pepper

Cut the lobster flesh into fingernail-size pieces. Melt the butter in a heavy-based pan, add the shallots, garlic and parsley and cook for 1 minute. Add the mustard, white wine and brandy and boil for 30 seconds to reduce the liquid slightly. Pour in the 150 ml (5 fl oz) cream and lemon juice. Stir well and add the lobster flesh and Parmesan. Bring the mixture to the boil, reduce the heat and allow to simmer for 1 minute. Season with salt and pepper to taste.

Spoon the lobster flesh into the shells and top with the sauce. Mix together the egg yolk and remaining 2 tablespoons cream and spoon over the sauce. Cook under a hot grill to brown the top quickly. Serve hot.

Fillets of Plaice served on a bed of Mangoes with Grilled Bananas

·❧·

This is an extremely classical recipe but has been adapted to suit modern tastes. The components of the dish might seem strange, but I can assure you that the marriage of flavours is fabulous. This recipe was devised after abducting a lady who had purchased a fistful of bananas. I think she had banana butties in mind! Serve with sauté potatoes and perhaps fresh spinach.

Serves 4

4 plaice fillets, 4 oz each, skinned
150 g (or 6 oz) butter
100 g (4 oz) plain flour
4 bananas
350 ml (12 fl oz) vegetable stock
1 garlic clove, crushed
1 tablespoon chopped fresh coriander
50 g (2 oz) shallots, chopped

1 tablespoon curry powder
120 ml (4 fl oz) dry white wine
50 ml (2 fl oz) double cream
4 tablespoons mango chutney
25 g (1 oz) grated coconut flesh
2 tablespoons chopped fresh dill
Salt and freshly ground black pepper

Season the fish fillets with salt and pepper. Melt 100 g (4 oz) of the butter. Coat the fish in 75 g (3 oz) of the flour, shake off surplus then dip them on both sides in the melted butter. Place on a grilling tray and set aside. Slice the bananas in half widthways at an angle of 45 degrees. Dip them in the coating flour and then in the butter. Place them on a flameproof dish.

Prepare the sauce by melting 25 g (1 oz) of butter in a pan. Add the remaining 25 g (1 oz) of flour and, stirring continuously, cook gently until it looks sandy in texture. Remove from the heat and gradually stir in the stock. Bring slowly to the boil and continue to cook, stirring, until the sauce thickens.

Heat the remaining 25 g (1 oz) butter in a pan, add the garlic, coriander and shallots and cook for 1 minute, then add the curry powder. Mix together and pour in the wine. Boil until reduced by half then add the sauce and mix together. Add the cream and season with salt and pepper to taste. Cover with a piece of greaseproof paper and keep warm.

Cook the fish and banana under the grill for about 5 minutes until the fish is tender and the bananas a golden brown. Spoon the mango chutney onto serving plates, place the fillets on top and cap each fillet with the grilled bananas. Dust the top of the bananas with the grated coconut flesh and chopped dill. Surround the fish with the sauce and serve hot.

Scampi in an Egg and Butter Sauce flavoured with Tarragon

To enjoy the flavours of this dish it is important to ensure that the sauce permeates the scampi, so don't be reluctant to combine the two. Browning the dish under a hot grill really enhances the presentation, but it is important to serve and eat the dish as soon after as possible. Accompany with Rice Pilaff (page 73).

Serves 4

2 tablespoons white wine vinegar
½ tablespoon water
6 peppercorns, crushed
15 g (½ oz) shallots, finely chopped
4 egg yolks
150 g (5 oz) clarified butter
Pinch of cayenne pepper

Juice of ¼ lemon
1 tablespoon chopped fresh tarragon
450 g (1 lb) scampi
A sprig of fresh parsley
1 small onion, finely chopped
50 ml (2 fl oz) double cream
225 g (8 oz) Rice Pilaff (page 73)
Salt and freshly ground black pepper

Put the wine vinegar, water, peppercorns and shallots in a pan and boil until reduced by half. Allow to cool then strain the liquid into a heatproof bowl and add the egg yolks. Sit the bowl over a pan of gently simmering water and whisk until the egg yolks double in volume. Gradually whisk in the clarified butter, a little at a time. Make sure that the bowl does not become too hot or the mixture will curdle. Season with salt, pepper and cayenne, and add the lemon juice and tarragon.

Put the scampi in a pan with enough water to cover, add the parsley, onion and a pinch of salt and cook for 5–10 minutes until tender. Once cooked, remove from the liquid and drain on kitchen paper. Mix the scampi into the sauce, add the cream and stir together. Arrange a border of rice pilaff in a flame-proof dish and put the scampi and sauce in the centre. Cook under a hot grill until golden brown. Serve immediately.

Rainbow Trout cooked in a Garlic and Caper Butter with Herring Roes

Trout cooked in butter produces the most wonderful aromas and taste when combined with these ingredients, especially the roe, and takes a lot of beating. Most good fishmongers will prepare the fish for you. If trout is not available then you could use any oily fish for this dish. Serve with boiled new potatoes.

Serves 4

8 fillets of rainbow trout, 175 g (6 oz) each
100 g (4 oz) plain flour
1 tablespoon chopped fennel leaves
1 tablespoon olive oil
100 g (4 oz) unsalted butter
3 garlic cloves, crushed
50 g (2 oz) shiitake mushrooms, sliced
25 g (1 oz) capers, finely chopped
8 herring roes
50 g (2 oz) white breadcrumbs
3 tablespoons chopped fresh parsley
Juice of 1 lemon
Salt and freshly ground black pepper
Fennel leaves, to garnish
8 lemon wedges, to garnish

Season the fish fillets with salt and pepper. Mix together the flour and fennel and use to coat the fillets, shaking off any surplus. Heat the oil in a large frying pan and add the butter. When melted, place the trout in the pan, best side down, and cook gently for 2 minutes. Carefully turn the fish over and continue cooking for 1–2 minutes until the fish is cooked. Remove from the pan onto a warmed serving dish, cover and keep warm.

Add the garlic, mushrooms and capers to the pan and cook gently for 3 minutes. Meanwhile, place the herring roes onto a grilling tray. Mix together the breadcrumbs and 1 tablespoon of parsley. Spoon a little of the garlic and caper butter over them, then sprinkle with the breadcrumbs and parsley. Cook under the grill for 5 minutes until golden brown.

Add the lemon juice and remaining chopped parsley to the remaining garlic butter. Pour the butter over the trout, place a herring roe on top of each fillet and garnish with the fennel leaves and lemon wedges.

Baked Casserole of Shellfish in a Sorrel and Dijon Mustard Sauce

Filo pastry is so widely used these days and, given how easy it is to use, it's no wonder. Providing you use really fresh shellfish and adhere to the rules for hygiene safety, then this is a super dish to prepare in advance and freeze until needed. I like to serve it with a dressed green salad.

Serves 4

180 g (7 oz) butter
40 g (1½ oz) plain flour
450 ml (15 fl oz) fish stock or milk
50 g (2 oz) shallots, finely chopped
1 teaspoon green peppercorns
3 tablespoons chopped sorrel
100 g (4 oz) prawns
50 g (2 oz) shelled mussels

100 g (4 oz) scallops, quartered
100 g (4 oz) chestnut mushrooms
1 garlic clove, crushed
1 tablespoon Dijon mustard
120 ml (4 fl oz) dry vermouth
5 sheets of filo pastry
Salt and freshly ground black pepper

Prepare the sauce by melting 40 g (1½ oz) of the butter in a heavy-based pan. Add the flour and, stirring continuously, cook until it looks sandy in texture. Remove from the heat and gradually stir in the stock or milk. Bring slowly to the boil and continue to cook, stirring, until the sauce thickens. Remove from the heat and cover with a piece of greaseproof paper.

Melt a further 40 g (1½ oz) of the butter in a pan, add the shallots and cook for minute. Add the peppercorns, sorrel, shellfish, mushrooms and garlic, cook for a further minute then add the mustard and vermouth. Season with salt and pepper to taste. Add the seafood mixture to the sauce and gently mix together.

Pre-heat the oven to 190°C/375°F/Gas 5.

Place a 20-cm (8-in) flan ring on a baking tray. Melt the remaining 100 g (4 oz) of butter. Brush the sheets of pastry with the butter, one at a time, and line the ring, letting the pastry fall over the sides of the tin. Spoon the shellfish mixture into the flan ring and fold over the edges of the pastry to the centre to cover the mixture. Brush the top of the pastry with butter. Bake for 10–15 minutes until golden brown. Carefully remove from the flan ring and serve hot.

Fillets of Sole filled with a Casserole of Oyster Mushrooms, Prawns and Smoked Salmon

— ❧❧❧ —

It is impossible to describe the aromas and flavours derived from using smoked salmon in a sauce. Suffice to say, it drives people crazy as I found out when, together with my hostage from Canterbury, we created this dish. Serve with fresh broccoli.

Serves 4

8 sole fillets, 4 oz each
50 g (2 oz) carrot, sliced
50 g (2 oz) celery, sliced
50 g (2 oz) white of leek, sliced
50 g (2 oz) onion, sliced
A sprig of fresh dill
175 ml (6 fl oz) dry white wine
550 ml (18 fl oz) water
Juice of 1 lemon
Salt and freshly ground black pepper

FOR THE FILLING:
25 g (1 oz) butter
100 g (4 oz) oyster mushrooms,
   finely chopped
50 g (2 oz) prawns
A sprig of fresh dill, finely chopped
Zest of ½ a lemon, finely chopped

FOR THE SAUCE:
300 ml (10 fl oz) double cream
150 ml (5 fl oz) yoghurt
Zest of ½ a lemon, finely sliced
Juice of ½ a lemon
25 g (1 oz) smoked salmon, finely
   sliced (or more, if you wish, of
   this luxury item!)

TO GARNISH:
Sprigs of fresh dill
Lemon wedges
75 g (3 oz) seedless grapes, skinned
   and chilled

Season the fish fillets with salt and pepper and fold them in third. Place in the fridge. Prepare the cooking liquid for the fish by putting the carrot, celery, leek, onion and dill into a shallow poaching pan. Add the wine, water and lemon juice and bring to the boil. Reduce the heat and simmer for 10 minutes.

Meanwhile, prepare the filling. Melt the butter in a pan, add the mushrooms, prawns, dill and lemon zest and cook gently for 1–2 minutes. Season with salt and pepper, cover and keep warm.

Remove the fish from the fridge, place into the cooking liquid, cover and simmer very gently for 4–6 minutes until tender. Leave the fish in the liquid until ready to serve. Pour one-third of the cooking liquid into a small pan and boil rapidly until it has reduced by half. Add the cream, yoghurt, lemon zest and lemon juice and bring to the boil. Finally, add the smoked salmon and season with salt and pepper.

Pour the sauce onto warmed serving plates, ensuring that each plate has an equal amount of smoked salmon. Using a slotted spoon, carefully remove the sole from the pan, and drain well. Place 2 fillets on each plate and insert a portion of the mushroom filling into each fillet. Serve garnished with the dill sprigs, lemon wedges and chilled grapes.

Lightly Creamed Scallops with a Salmon Caviar Sauce

❧❀❧

Of all the seafoods available, for me the king has to be scallops. They are so delightful to look at, cook and eat. The salmon caviar works particularly well with this dish, but if it doesn't appeal, or you are unable to obtain it, then simply miss it out. Serve with a salad of crisp summer leaves.

Serves 6

400 g (14 oz) scallops
1 egg
1 egg white
50 ml (2 fl oz) double cream
1 tablespoon snipped fresh chives
2 tablespoons salmon caviar
3 tablespoons water
3 tablespoons white wine vinegar
25 g (1 oz) shallots, finely chopped

225 g (8 oz) unsalted butter, at
    room temperature
2 tablespoons lemon juice
1 tablespoon finely chopped fresh
    chervil
Salt and freshly ground black pepper
3 large tomatoes, skinned, seeded
    and finely chopped, to garnish
12 leaves of chervil, to garnish

Purée the scallops in a food processor. Add the egg and egg white, process for 2 minutes, then chill for 40 minutes.

Pre-heat the oven to 200°C/400°F/Gas 6.

Lightly oil 6 dariole moulds. Return the mixture to the food processor, add the cream and process for 2–3 seconds until the mixture is thick and creamy. Be careful not to overdo at this stage. Season with salt and pepper. Add the chives and, using a metal spoon, mix lightly together.

Spoon half the mixture into the prepared moulds so that it comes halfway up the moulds. Using half the caviar, place a little in the centre of each and then top with the remaining mixture. Cover each mousse with a piece of greaseproof paper then cover with foil. Stand the moulds in a roasting tin then pour in enough hot water to come halfway up the sides of the moulds. Bake for 25–30 minutes until firm. They should feel springy to the touch.

To make the sauce, put the water, wine vinegar and shallots in a pan and boil until reduced by two-thirds. Leave to cool slightly. Gradually whisk in two-thirds of the butter, a small piece at a time. Return the sauce to a very low heat, whisk harder and add the remaining butter. Season with pepper and add the lemon juice, the remaining caviar and the chervil. Do not reboil.

Flood a little of the sauce onto individual serving plates. Carefully turn out the mousses onto the centre of each plate. Garnish with a small heap of the tomato flesh and chervil leaves.

Mussels in a Light Saffron Broth

Saffron gives a lovely finish to this dish, it harmonizes beautifully with the colour of the mussels. This was created for a large family and all that's needed is a large bowl containing the cooked mussels and some warm crusty French bread. Oh yes, I nearly forgot, and a large bottle of chilled white wine!

Serves 2

2.25 litres (2 quarts) mussels
250 ml (8 fl oz) dry white wine
50 g (2 oz) shallots, chopped
2 garlic cloves, crushed
1 bay leaf
4 fennel leaves
1 tablespoon chopped fresh parsley
Pinch of saffron

150 ml (5 fl oz) cream
100 g (4 oz) butter
2 tomatoes, skinned, seeded and
    chopped
25 g (1 oz) cooked long-grain rice
1 tablespoon snipped fresh chives
Juice of ½ a lemon
Salt and freshly ground black pepper

Clean the mussels by removing the beard, scrubbing and washing in cold water. Pour the wine into a wide, deep pan and add the shallots, garlic, bay, fennel and parsley. Bring to the boil and tip in the mussels. Cover with a tight-fitting lid. Cook the mussels over a medium heat for 5–6 minutes, shaking the pan frequently. At this point it is important to discard any mussels that have not opened. Transfer the opened mussels to a warmed dish, cover with a lid and keep warm.

Strain the cooking liquid through a fine sieve into a clean pan and place over a high heat until reduced by about one-third. Reduce the heat and add the saffron and cream. Whisk in the butter, a small piece at a time, taking great care not to allow the sauce to curdle. Add the tomatoes, cooked rice, chives and lemon juice. Season to taste with salt and pepper. Pour the broth over the mussels and serve hot.

Roast Sea Bass served with Herb-crumbed Garlic and a Rich Red Wine and Mushroom Sauce

For this dish to work you really do need the elephant garlic, so this is one where I wouldn't recommend you substitute the ingredient for something else. Be patient, search out the ingredient – it's worth the wait. Serve with a tomato and basil salad.

Serves 4

16 elephant garlic cloves
75 g (3 oz) plain flour
1 tablespoon finely chopped fresh dill
1 tablespoon finely chopped fresh coriander
1 egg, beaten
175 g (6 oz) white breadcrumbs
4 fillets of sea bass, with the skin left on, 175 g (6 oz) each
2 tablespoons olive oil
Oil, for deep frying

50 g (2 oz) shallots, finely chopped
50 g (2 oz) oyster mushrooms, sliced
½ teaspoon crushed black pepper corns
150 ml (5 fl oz) red wine
150 ml (5 fl oz) fish, chicken or vegetable stock
100 g (4 oz) unsalted butter, cubed and chilled
Salt
Coriander leaves, to garnish

Put the garlic cloves in a pan, cover with cold water, bring to the boil and simmer for 1 minute. Drain the garlic, refresh under cold water and repeat the process twice. On the third boiling, test to ensure that the cloves are tender. If not, allow to cook for a little longer.

Skin the cloves. Mix the flour, dill and coriander together and put on a plate. Coat the garlic cloves in the flour mixture, beaten egg and finally the breadcrumbs. Set aside.

Pre-heat the oven to 230°C/450°F/Gas 8.

Make 3 incisions across the skin of the fish and then dip the fillets in the flour, shaking off the surplus. Heat the 2 tablespoons of oil in a heavy-based frying pan or roasting dish. Season the fish with salt and place the fillets, skin side down, into the hot oil. Allow to colour then carefully turn them over. Bake for 3–5 minutes until cooked.

Heat the oil in a deep-fat fryer and cook the garlic cloves for 10–12 minutes until golden brown. Drain on kitchen paper and keep hot.

Remove the fish from the pan and keep warm. Add the shallots to the pan and cook until soft but not coloured. Add the mushrooms and peppercorns and cook for a further 1 minute. Pour in the red wine and stock, and boil until reduced by half. Reduce the heat then gradually whisk in the chilled butter, a little at a time.

Flood 4 warmed serving plates with the sauce. Place the sea bass in the centre of each plate and surround it with the garlic cloves. Serve garnished with coriander leaves.

Peppered Fish Cakes with a Hot Tomato and Basil Chutney

Traditional fish cakes are so easy to make and so good to eat. This recipe is for those who enjoy their food slightly spicy and a little hot. The moistness of the tomatoes, coupled with the basil, takes some of the sting out of the dish.

Serves 4

225 g (8 oz) skinned cod fillets
450 g (1 lb) old potatoes, cooked
   and mashed
75 g (3 oz) butter, softened
50 g (2 oz) anchovies, finely chopped
1 large green pepper, seeded and
   finely chopped
3 tablespoons chopped fresh parsley
2 egg yolks
100 g (4 oz) breadcrumbs
1 tablespoon finely crushed black
   peppercorns
100 g (4 oz) plain flour
2 eggs, lightly beaten
50 ml (2 fl oz) olive oil

8 large firm tomatoes, skinned,
   seeded and roughly chopped
4 garlic cloves, crushed
75 g (3 oz) shallots, finely chopped
4 tablespoons chopped fresh basil
2 tablespoons tomato purée
Juice of ½ a lemon
1 tablespoon Worcestershire sauce
1 teaspoon Tabasco sauce
Pinch of sugar
Salt and freshly ground black pepper
Olive oil, for frying
Selection of salad leaves, finely
   chopped
8 small basil leaves, to garnish

Season the cod fillets with salt and pepper and steam for 6 minutes until just tender. Using a fork, flake the flesh into small pieces and add to the mashed potato. Mix in the butter, anchovies, green pepper, 1 tablespoon of the parsley and the egg yolks. Season with salt and a little pepper. Divide into 8 equal pieces and chill for at least 30 minutes.

Mix together the breadcrumbs, peppercorns and remaining 2 tablespoons of parsley and put on a plate. Put the flour and beaten eggs onto 2 separate plates. Coat each piece of fish mixture with the flour, egg and finally the breadcrumbs. Shape the fish cakes and chill again.

Heat the olive oil in a pan, add the tomatoes, garlic and shallots and cook gently for 2 minutes. Continue cooking while adding the basil, tomato purée and lemon juice. Season with Worcestershire sauce, Tabasco, sugar, salt and pepper. Remove from the heat, cover and keep warm.

Heat sufficient olive oil in a large frying pan and carefully fry the fish cakes on both sides for about 5 minutes until golden brown. Remove from the pan and drain on kitchen paper. Using the chopped salad leaves, form a circle on 4 serving plates, leaving sufficient room for 2 fish cakes to be presented in the centre. Spoon the tomato and basil chutney onto the centre of each plate and place the fish cakes on top. Serve garnished with the basil leaves.

POULTRY AND GAME

There is no doubt that if the main ingredient is of poor quality, the finished quality of the dish itself, no matter how lovingly you prepare it, will not improve with cooking. It really is worth spending a little time, effort and expense in order to seek out the shops which sell well-fed chicken, duck and game that have been correctly dressed and hung.

As for cooking, I'm afraid I remain adamant that poultry must be thoroughly cooked and that it needs a short resting period after cooking and prior to being served. This allows the flesh to relax and ensures its tenderness.

In general terms poultry represents really good value for money but it's most important to know what to look for when purchasing so that you acquire the best available. A 3½-lb chicken is large enough to feed a family of four and when in prime condition it has firm plump breasts, well-rounded thighs and a slightly pink tinge to the skin which should be complete and not bruised or torn.

The mass-produced chickens tend to be lacking in flavour and the flesh is often too soft, making them boring to eat. The advantage is that they really are cheap. But you get what you pay for and for a few 'shillings' more you could get a plump corn-fed chicken which oozes taste and texture.

There are various types and sizes of poultry and for chickens they begin as poussin, which weigh between 8–10 oz, cockerel 10–18 oz, young chicken, referred to in French as *poulet de grain*, 2–2½ lb, chicken 3–3½ lb, boiling fowl 4–6 lb, young fat chicken 2–3 lb, capon 5–8 lb and fat chicken 4–8 lb.

Game falls into two categories: 'furred' or 'feathered'. All furred game, after hanging, should be marinated, usually for 24 hours. This will develop the distinct flavour of the flesh. Due to the lack of fat in most game it is advisable to add extra fat over the meat or insert it inside the flesh in order to prevent it being too dry after cooking. Hoofed game is at its best between 4–5 years of age, the fat should be bright and clear and the cleft of the hoof smooth and closed.

Feathered game is very much a seasonal commodity. Pheasants are available between October and December, partridge between September and October, grouse between 11 August and December and woodcock between September and April. But as with everything today, these items, along with many others, are in the shops all year round, thanks to the deep freeze. All feathered game improves dramatically by hanging for a few days in a cool well-ventilated area.

Cromesquis

———————— ⋅⋙⋘⋅ ————————

This is, without a doubt, one of the tastiest and most interesting ways to serve left-over chicken. The recipe will work with any left-over cooked meat. It's especially nice if you serve it with a fresh tomato and black olive sauce.

Serves 4

15 g (½ oz) butter
15 g (½ oz) plain flour
150 ml (5 fl oz) hot chicken stock
150 g (5 oz) cooked chicken, finely
    chopped
50 g (2 oz) cooked tongue, finely
    chopped
15 g (½ oz) cooked mushrooms,
    finely chopped
1 egg yolk

8 slices of bacon
Oil, for deep frying
Salt and freshly ground black pepper

FOR THE BATTER:
5 g (⅙ oz) fresh yeast
150 ml (5 fl oz) water
100 g (4 oz) plain flour
150 ml (5 fl oz) oil
15 g (½ oz) sugar

To make the batter, blend the yeast with 1 tablespoon of the water until smooth. Whisk the remaining ingredients together and add the yeast liquid. Cover and leave to rise in a warm place for 1 hour.

Melt the butter in a pan, add the flour and mix to form a roux. Remove from the heat and gradually stir in the stock until smooth. Bring slowly to the boil and cook, stirring constantly, until the sauce boils and thickens. Add the chicken, tongue and mushrooms and cook gently for a further 5 minutes. Remove from the heat, then add the egg yolk and season with salt and pepper to taste. Turn the mixture onto a lightly greased tray and chill for 2 hours.

Divide the mixture into 8 equal pieces and, with lightly floured hands, mould into croquette shapes. Wrap a piece of bacon around each one then dip in the batter. Heat the oil in a deep-fat fryer to 180°C/350°F. Place a few croquettes at a time into the oil and fry for 3–4 minutes until golden brown. Drain on kitchen paper and serve hot.

Chicken and Ham Cutlets

———————— ❧❧❧ ————————

This is a great recipe because it allows you to prepare the cutlets the day
before you intend to eat them. In fact, the best advice is to buy
a huge chicken, one that is far too big for your needs, roast it, eat
what you need and convert the rest into cutlets.

Serves 4

15 g (½ oz) butter	*1 egg yolk*
90 g (3½ oz) plain flour	*2 eggs, lightly beaten*
120 ml (4 fl oz) chicken stock	*75 g (3 oz) fresh white breadcrumbs*
225 g (8 oz) cooked chicken, finely chopped	*Oil, for shallow frying*
100 g (4 oz) cooked ham, finely chopped	*Salt and freshly ground black pepper*
	1 tablespoon chopped fresh parsley, to garnish

Melt the butter in a pan, add 15 g (½ oz) of the flour and cook gently until the
roux looks sandy in texture. Remove from the heat and gradually stir in the
stock until smooth. Bring slowly to the boil, stirring constantly, until the sauce
boils and thickens. Add the chicken and ham to the sauce and season with salt
and pepper to taste. Allow to cool slightly and then mix in the egg yolk and chill
for 2 hours.

Divide the mixture into 8 equal pieces then, with lightly floured hands,
mould into cutlet shapes. Dip each cutlet in the remaining 75 g (3 oz) of flour,
then in the eggs and finally coat with the breadcrumbs. Heat a little oil in a
frying pan and cook for 3–5 minutes on each side until golden. Serve garnished
with a little chopped parsley.

Hungarian Chicken Suprême

❦

The combination of paprika and tomato gives a lovely colour to this chicken dish and the sediment left in the frying pan after the meat has been cooked will enhance the flavour of the sauce.

Serves 4

4 boneless chicken breasts, 4 oz each
75 g (3 oz) butter
1 tablespoon olive oil
50 g (2 oz) shallots, finely chopped
1 garlic clove, crushed
175 ml (6 fl oz) white wine
1 tablespoon paprika

3 tomatoes, skinned, seeded and chopped
1 tablespoon fresh basil, shredded
175 ml (6 fl oz) double cream
Salt and freshly ground black pepper
Rice Pilaff (page 73), to serve

Put the chicken breasts between 2 sheets of greaseproof paper or in a polythene bag and, using a wooden rolling pin, lightly beat them to an even thickness. Heat the butter and oil in a large frying pan, add the breasts, season with salt and pepper and cook gently on both sides for about 20 minutes until tender and cooked right through. Remove from the pan, cover and keep warm.

Put the shallots and garlic into the pan and cook for 3–5 minutes until soft. Drain off any surplus fat, then add the wine, paprika, chopped tomatoes and basil. Cook for a further 2 minutes, then add the cream. Bring to the boil and season with salt and pepper.

Place a serving of the rice onto serving plates. Slice the chicken breast into 4 pieces, arrange around the rice and pour over the sauce.

Breast of Chicken stuffed with Spinach and Mushrooms

❧❀❧

The origins of this dish belong to Jean Yves Morel and the key to its success is in leaving the chicken to rest for at least 10 minutes after cooking and before serving.

Serves 4

4 boneless chicken breasts, 4 oz each	*120 ml (4 fl oz) dry vermouth*
75 g (3 oz) butter	*25 g (1 oz) shallots, finely chopped*
225 g (8 oz) spinach, chopped	*100 g (4 oz) unsalted butter*
100 g (4 oz) mushrooms, sliced	*1 tablespoon chopped fresh tarragon*
Pinch of freshly grated nutmeg	*Salt and freshly ground black pepper*

Using a sharp knife, make an incision lengthways in the chicken breasts to form pockets. Melt 25 g (1 oz) of the butter in a pan, add the spinach and mushrooms and fry for 2–3 minutes until tender. Season with nutmeg, salt and pepper. Remove from the heat and leave to cool.

Season the chicken breasts with salt and pepper. Spoon the spinach and mushroom mixture into the pockets and secure with cocktail sticks.

Heat the remaining 50 g (2 oz) of butter in a frying pan, add the chicken breasts and cook gently for about 5–8 minutes until thoroughly cooked. Remove from the pan, cover and keep warm.

Add the vermouth and shallots to the pan and boil rapidly until reduced to one-third. Reduce the heat and gradually whisk in the unsalted butter a small piece at a time. Stir in the chopped tarragon.

Slice the chicken breasts and arrange neatly in a circle on serving plates. Pour over the sauce and serve.

Chicken braised in a Red Wine Sauce

A truly authentic peasant approach to cooking chicken. No fuss, no frills, just a huge pan of flavour. Each ingredient enhances the other. I like to keep a bowl of the sauce to eat the following day as a soup!

Serves 4

1.5 kg (3½ lb) chicken or 8 chicken portions
75 g (3 oz) butter
5 tablespoons olive oil
175 g (6 oz) streaky bacon, finely chopped
2 garlic cloves, crushed
12 button mushrooms

12 shallots
600 ml (1 pint) red wine
1 bouquet garni
1 tablespoon cornflour
4 slices of bread, crusts removed and cut into quarters
Salt

Joint the chicken into 8 pieces. Melt the butter in a large frying pan, add 1 tablespoon of the oil and, when hot, add the chicken pieces and seal on all sides. Add the bacon and garlic, cook for 1 minute, then add the mushrooms and shallots. Cook for a further 1 minute, pour in the wine and add the bouquet garni. Cover and simmer gently for 30 minutes until the chicken pieces are tender.

Remove the chicken pieces, vegetables and bouquet garni from the sauce. Cover and keep warm. Increase the heat under the pan and reduce the wine to one-third. Blend the cornflour with a little cold water, then whisk it into the wine. Season with a little salt and return the chicken pieces and the vegetables to the sauce.

Heat the remaining 4 tablespoons of oil in a frying pan, add the bread and fry quickly until golden. Drain on kitchen paper and arrange them on serving plates. Place a piece of chicken onto each croûton (fried bread) and cover with the sauce.

Ballotines of Chicken

I have fond memories of this dish as it was cooked with a lovely family which consisted of Mum, Dad and four children. The legs were huge and, in fact, two legs fed the whole family, leaving the breasts for the following day. It is without doubt a real old-fashioned, full-flavour recipe. Well worth the effort.

Serves 4

4 chicken legs, 100 g (4 oz) each
225 g (8 oz) sausagemeat
50 g (2 oz) butter, diced
50 g (2 oz) carrots, finely chopped
50 g (2 oz) leeks, finely chopped
50 g (2 oz) onions, finely chopped
50 g (2 oz) celery, finely chopped
25 g (1 oz) streaky bacon, finely chopped

50 g (2 oz) plain flour
1 tablespoon tomato purée
175 ml (6 fl oz) red wine
600 ml (1 pint) chicken stock
1 bouquet garni
Salt and freshly ground black pepper

Remove the bone from the chicken legs, without opening the drumstick flesh, by scraping the flesh away from the bone with just the tip of a sharp knife. Stuff the legs with the sausagemeat, reshape and then secure with string.

Pre-heat the oven to 180°C/350°F/Gas 4.

Heat the butter in a flameproof casserole dish, add the chicken drumsticks, season with salt and pepper and brown on all sides. Remove from the casserole dish and put aside. Add the vegetables and bacon, cook for 2 minutes, then stir in the flour and mix well. Add the tomato purée and red wine, then gradually stir in the stock. Bring to the boil, stirring, then return the chicken legs to the sauce. Add the bouquet garni. Cover and bake for 40–45 minutes until the chicken legs are tender.

Remove the string from the chicken legs. Strain the sauce into a pan then boil rapidly until reduced to a sauce that will lightly coat the chicken legs. Pour the sauce over the ballotines and serve.

Chicken and Mushroom Pie

❧❀❧

There are occasions in life when only a chicken and mushroom pie will help. This is comfort food. It's all to do with taking you back to your early days through flavours and tastes, and this recipe will do just that.

Serves 4

1.75 kg (4 lb) chicken or 8 chicken
  portions
75 g (3 oz) butter
100 g (4 oz) rindless back bacon
225 g (8 oz) button onions
175 g (6 oz) button mushrooms

350 g (12 oz) potatoes, diced
300 ml (10 fl oz) chicken stock
1 tablespoon chopped fresh tarragon
225 g (8 oz) puff pastry
Beaten egg, to glaze
Salt and freshly ground black pepper

Joint the chicken into 8 pieces. Melt the butter in a frying pan, add the chicken pieces and seal on all sides. Season with salt and pepper. Remove from the pan. Wrap a piece of bacon around each joint of chicken and place into an ovenproof pie dish. Add the remaining ingredients except the pastry and the beaten egg.

Pre-heat the oven to 200°C/400°F/Gas 6.

On a lightly floured surface, roll out the pastry until about 2.5 cm (1 in) larger all round than the pie dish. Cut off a strip from all around the edge of the pastry, then place the strip on the rim of the pie dish. Moisten with water then place the pastry lid on top. Press the edge together to seal and make a small hole in the centre. Brush with beaten egg. Bake for about 40 minutes until golden brown. Serve hot.

Fricassee of Turkey

It's such a shame that turkey has the reputation of being eaten only at Christmas as, in many respects, people avoid buying it for the rest of the year. Most supermarkets sell turkey breasts and they are not only really tasty but also economical.

Serves 4

75 g (3 oz) butter
450 g (1 lb) cooked turkey, chopped
1 tablespoon chopped fresh coriander
40 g (1½ oz) plain flour
450 ml (15 fl oz) chicken stock

225 g (8 oz) button onions
100 g (4 oz) button mushrooms
150 ml (5 fl oz) double cream
2 egg yolks
Salt and freshly ground black pepper

Pre-heat the oven to 200°C/400°F/Gas 6.

Melt the butter in a deep ovenproof pan, add the turkey and coriander and season with salt and pepper. Dust with the flour and mix well together. Gradually add the stock, stirring, then add the onions and mushrooms.

Bake in the oven for 35–40 minutes until thoroughly heated through.

Using a slotted spoon, remove the turkey and vegetables from the sauce and keep warm in a serving dish. Mix together the cream and egg yolks, add a little of the hot sauce, mix well then add to the sauce. Remove from the heat and pour over the turkey. Serve immediately.

Turkey and Peppers in a Cream and Sherry Sauce

❦

This is a lovely way to serve left-over turkey (or chicken) but do please
be sure to follow the guidelines for the use of pre-cooked meats, namely
that the meat must be chilled and not left out in a warm environment
and the meat must be thoroughly reheated.
Serve with buttered noodles.

Serves 4

65 g (2½ oz) butter
15 g (½ oz) plain flour
300 ml (10 fl oz) hot chicken stock
1 green pepper, seeded and cut into
 strips
1 red pepper, seeded and cut into
 strips
1 small onion, finely chopped
1 clove garlic, crushed

50 g (2 oz) sweetcorn
75 g (3 oz) mushrooms, sliced
450 g (1 lb) cooked turkey, cut into
 strips
4 tablespoons sherry
150 ml (5 fl oz) double cream
Salt and freshly ground black pepper
4 portions cooked noodles, to serve

Melt 15 g (½ oz) of the butter in a pan, add the flour and mix to form a roux.
Remove from the heat and gradually stir in the stock until smooth. Bring slowly
to the boil and cook, stirring constantly, until the sauce boils and thickens.
Season with salt and pepper to taste.

Melt the remaining 50 g (2 oz) of butter in a pan, add the vegetables and
cook for 5 minutes, stirring constantly. Stir in the sauce and turkey and cook
until the turkey is thoroughly reheated. Stir in the sherry and cream. Check the
seasoning and adjust, if necessary, before serving.

Marinated Grilled Duckling Breasts with Green Cabbage and Ginger

❦

If you overcook the duckling breasts it is quite likely that the meat will become tough, so a careful eye is the order of the day. When serving this, cut the meat at a slight angle. This gives the appearance of there being more on the plate than there really is. It is also essential to let the meat rest for a while before carving. This dish is good served with rösti or sauté potatoes.

Serves 4

4 large boneless duckling breasts (either Aylesbury or Barbary), 175 g (6 oz) each
1 tablespoon groundnut or vegetable oil

FOR THE MARINADE:
4 tablespoons clear honey
50 g (2 oz) shallots, chopped
4 tablespoons grated fresh root ginger
4 tablespoons olive oil
4 tablespoons dry sherry
4 tablespoons soy sauce
Salt and freshly ground black pepper

FOR THE SAUCE:
275 ml (9 fl oz) brown veal stock
4 tablespoons dry sherry
75 g (3 oz) butter
300 ml (10 fl oz) chicken stock

FOR THE VEGETABLES:
1 carrot
1 stick celery
1 leek
1 tablespoon vegetable oil
2.5-cm (1-in) piece of fresh root ginger, finely chopped
1 small garlic clove, finely chopped
½ a medium cabbage, finely sliced

Mix all the marinade ingredients together. Using a sharp knife, score the skin of the duckling breasts into thin slices (not the meat). Place the duckling breasts in the marinade and leave in a cool place for 12 hours. Dry the marinated duckling breasts with kitchen paper and season with salt. Reserve the marinade. Heat the oil in a frying pan until very hot, carefully add the duckling breasts, skin-side down, and leave the pan very hot for about 3 minutes until the skin is black. Keep control of the temperature, but do not worry about the smoke.

Turn over the duckling breasts, leave for 1 minute then remove the excess fat. Place the pan under a grill for about 8 minutes until slightly pink and a firm texture. Pour off the fat in the pan and grill the duckling breasts in the pan for a further 20 minutes until cooked but still slightly pink.

Meanwhile, make the sauce. Put the stock into a frying pan. Add the reserved marinade and the sherry. Add the butter and boil until the sauce is reduced to one-third. Season to taste with salt and pepper.

Cut the carrot, celery and leek into julienne strips. Blanch in boiling water then drain. Heat the vegetable oil in a pan, add the ginger and garlic and fry for 2–3 minutes until they begin to colour. Add the shredded cabbage and a little chicken stock to moisten. Cover and cook for about 2 minutes until tender. Place a little of the warm julienne of vegetables in the middle of each serving plate. Slice the duckling breasts and arrange on top. Add a mound of cabbage to each plate and pour around some of the sauce.

Braised Breasts of Barbary Duckling served with Roasted Shallots and Garlic

For this recipe I persuaded my shopper to roast the shallots, with the skin left on, as an accompaniment to the duckling and watched with interest as he teased the shallots from the skins in order to eat them. As for the duckling, it really does need to remain pink for serving.

Serves 2

2 Barbary duckling breasts,
    6 oz each
2 tablespoons oil
50 g (2 oz) onion, chopped
50 g (2 oz) leek, chopped
50 g (2 oz) celery, chopped
50 g (2 oz) carrot, chopped
300 ml (10 fl oz) rich duck stock
1 tablespoon oil, preferably almond
100 g (4 oz) shallots

8 garlic cloves
50 g (2 oz) fresh root ginger, finely
    chopped
2 tablespoons clear honey
1 tablespoon finely chopped mixed
    fresh herbs
175 ml (6 fl oz) red wine
50 g (2 oz) butter
Salt and freshly ground black pepper
Sprigs of fresh coriander, to garnish

Season the duckling breasts with salt and pepper. Heat the oil in a frying pan, add the breasts and cook for 2–3 minutes on each side to seal.

Meanwhile, in a separate frying pan, heat the almond oil, add the shallots and garlic and cook for 3–5 minutes until tender. Remove from the pan and add the onion, leek, celery and carrot. Add the stock and return the duckling breasts to the pan. Simmer for 5–8 minutes until the breasts are tender. Remove from the pan and add the ginger, honey and herbs. Allow to cook to a glaze, stir in the red wine and mix well together.

Remove the duckling breasts from the pan and keep warm. Stir the butter into the sauce, then strain the sauce over the ginger and honey glaze. Check, and, if necessary, adjust the seasoning. Carve the duckling breasts and arrange on serving plates. Surround with the shallots and garlic, pour over the sauce and serve garnished with coriander sprigs.

Mousselines of Guinea Fowl with an Asparagus Sauce

❧❀❧

This is a lovely way of allowing all the flavour of the bird to be released whilst enjoying the most delicate mousseline possible. The dish was created for a shopper with fresh asparagus in her trolley, but I had spied a guinea fowl from the next counter. She, along with many others I suspect, had never eaten guinea fowl. You could use any white meat in place of the fowl and it would work just as well.

Serves 4

1 guinea fowl, about 750–900 g
(1½–2 lb) in weight
1 egg white
300 ml (10 fl oz) double cream
600 ml (1 pint) hot chicken stock
40 g (1½ oz) butter

40 g (1½ oz) plain flour
175 g (6 oz) asparagus, cooked
50 ml (2 fl oz) double cream
Salt and freshly ground black pepper
Chopped fresh coriander, to garnish

Remove the flesh from the guinea fowl then purée in a food processor. Add the egg white and season with salt and pepper. Beat until it becomes stiff and gelatinous. Push the mixture through a fine sieve, then chill for 1 hour.

Pre-heat the oven to 180°C/350°F/Gas 4.

Lightly butter a shallow baking tin. Beat the cream into the mixture, taking great care not to curdle it. Using 2 tablespoons, mould the mixture into 8–12 egg shapes and place them onto the prepared tin.

Pour the hot stock into the tin, cover with greaseproof paper and bake for about 15 minutes until set.

Meanwhile, beat together the butter and flour to make a beurre manié. When the mousselines are cooked, very carefully drain the liquid into a pan. Bring the stock to the boil and then gradually whisk in the beurre manié. Add the cooked asparagus, cream and season with salt and pepper.

Place the mousselines onto serving plates, coat with the sauce and serve garnished with the coriander.

Roast Goose with a Calvados and Prune Stuffing

This is a special occasion dish. There is nothing fancy in this recipe, no silly
sickly sauces, just pure flavour and a stunning stuffing. The recipe will scale
down quite successfully for a smaller bird or, alternatively, you could make
all of the stuffing and cook some of it wrapped in foil separately in the oven,
to eat the following day – it's that good! If you fancy, serve with a little
apple sauce and, of course, roast potatoes and green vegetables.

Serves 8–10

4.5 kg (10 lb) goose and its giblets

FOR THE STUFFING:
50 g (2 oz) butter
275 g (10 oz) onions, finely chopped
50 g (2 oz) streaky bacon, finely
    chopped
100 g (4 oz) prunes, soaked and
    finely chopped
2 tablespoons chopped fresh sage
1 tablespoon chopped fresh coriander
225 g (8 oz) soft white breadcrumbs
2 eggs, lightly beaten
1 teaspoon crushed black peppercorns
3 tablespoons calvados

FOR THE GRAVY:
75 g (3 oz) onions
75 g (3 oz) celery
75 g (3 oz) carrots
75 g (3 oz) leeks
4 tablespoons sherry
1 bouquet garni
1.2 litres (2 pints) water
1 tablespoon arrowroot
Salt and freshly ground black pepper

Remove the giblets from the goose and set aside. Finely chop the goose liver.
Wash the bird and pat it dry with kitchen paper.

Pre-heat the oven to 220°C/425°F/Gas 7.

To make the stuffing, melt the butter in a large pan, add the onions and cook
for 5 minutes without browning. Add the bacon and goose liver and cook very
slowly for 10 minutes. Mix in the prunes, sage, coriander and breadcrumbs.
Remove from the heat, then add the eggs, black peppercorns and calvados.
Season with salt.

Stuff the rear end of the bird with the stuffing and, using either string or
wooden skewers, seal the end. Using a fork, prick the skin and then season with

salt and pepper. Bake for 45 minutes. Reduce the oven temperature to 180°C/350°F/Gas 4 and bake for a further 3½ hours until cooked. (It is important to drain off the fat in the roasting tin during cooking.)

Meanwhile, make the gravy. Pour a little boiling water over the giblets to scald them. Drain and put in a pan. Add the vegetables, sherry, bouquet garni and water and simmer for 1½ hours. Strain and reserve the stock.

Blend the arrowroot with a little cold water and whisk it into the stock. Bring to the boil, stirring, then season with salt and pepper to taste.

Carve the goose. Serve with the stuffing and the clear gravy.

Quail with Grapes in a Marsala Sauce

These delicious birds are often available ready-cleaned in most good supermarkets. I like to serve a crisp, well-dressed salad with mine, as well as a dish of sauté potatoes.

Serves 4

8 quails
75 g (3 oz) butter, melted
225 g (8 oz) seedless grapes, skinned
300 ml (10 fl oz) dry white wine

300 ml (10 fl oz) thickened gravy
(left over from the Sunday roast)
4 tablespoons Marsala
Juice of ½ a lemon
Salt and freshly ground black pepper

Pre-heat the oven to 220°C/425°F/Gas 7.

Season the quails with salt and pepper, put into a casserole dish and cover with the melted butter. Cover and cook in the oven for 20 minutes. Remove the lid and cook for a further 5 minutes to allow them to colour. You will need to baste the quails at least twice during this stage. Transfer the quails to a deep serving dish, add the grapes, cover and keep warm.

Place the casserole onto the stove and heat gently for 2 minutes. Carefully pour off the excess fat. Add the wine and boil to reduce by half then add the gravy and return to the boil. Using a wooden spoon, remove the sediment from the bottom of the pan. Add the Marsala and lemon juice. Season with salt and pepper to taste then strain the sauce over the quails before serving.

Breast of Pigeon served with a Port and Juniper Berry Sauce

✤

Be careful to check that all the shot has been removed before you begin cooking! Serve with creamed potatoes and a little freshly cooked broccoli.

Serves 4

4 pigeon breasts, 75–100 g (3–4 oz) each	25 g (1 oz) plain flour
175 g (6 oz) butter	1 tablespoon redcurrant jelly
50 g (2 oz) celery, chopped	150 ml (5 fl oz) red wine
50 g (2 oz) carrot, chopped	150 ml (5 fl oz) chicken stock
50 g (2 oz) leek, chopped	16 juniper berries
4 rashers of streaky bacon	150 ml (5 fl oz) port
	Salt and freshly ground black pepper

Pre-heat the oven to 220°C/425 °F/Gas 7.

Season the pigeon breasts with salt and pepper. Heat 75 g (3 oz) of the butter in a flameproof casserole dish, add the breasts and cook until sealed on both sides. Remove from the pan. Add the chopped vegetables, cook for 5 minutes then place the breasts on top of the vegetables. Cover with the bacon and cook in the oven for 15–20 minutes until tender.

Remove the breasts from the casserole dish, carefully pour off the surplus fat and place the casserole onto the stove. Add the flour and mix together. Cook for 2 minutes, stirring constantly. Add the redcurrant jelly then gradually stir in the red wine and chicken stock. Bring to the boil, stirring, then add the juniper berries and port. Simmer for 12–15 minutes until slightly thickened. Strain the sauce then gradually whisk in the remaining butter. Season with salt and pepper. Pour over the pigeon and serve.

Pheasant with a Normandy Sauce

— ✦❧❦✦ —

The hen pheasant is a much nicer bird for this dish because of its finer flavour. Be sure to have your supplier pluck and draw it for you – it saves an awful lot of effort.

Serves 2

2 tablespoons olive oil
75 g (3 oz) smoked bacon, finely chopped
75 g (3 oz) onion, finely chopped
2 garlic cloves, crushed
1 teaspoon crushed black pepper corns

4 cooking apples, peeled and quartered
1 hen pheasant, about 750 g (1½ lb)
150 ml (5 fl oz) dry cider
300 ml (10 fl oz) double cream
1 tablespoon chopped fresh coriander
Salt and freshly ground black pepper

Pre-heat the oven to 180°C/350°F/Gas 4.

Heat the oil in a pan. Add the bacon and onion and cook for 1 minute then add the garlic and crushed peppercorns. Cook for a further 5 minutes then remove from the pan. Add the apple quarters to the fat remaining in the pan and cook for 2 minutes then add to the cooked onion.

Add the pheasant to the pan and brown all over in the hot oil. Season with salt and pepper. Transfer to a casserole dish and add the onion and apple mixture.

Pour the cider into a pan and boil until reduced by half. Add the cream, season with salt and pepper and bring slowly to the boil. Pour over the pheasant. Add the coriander, cover and cook in the oven for between 35–40 minutes until the pheasant is tender.

Transfer the bird to a warmed serving dish. Blend the sauce in a food processor until smooth. Joint the pheasant and serve with the sauce poured over.

Rich Rabbit Stew with Baby Vegetables and Herb Dumplings

⋆⋆⋆

This classically English dish is further enhanced by the addition of the dumplings, which not only add interest to the finished presentation but also taste wonderful.

Serves 4

10 rabbit legs, skinned
About 50 g (2 oz) plain flour
6 tablespoons olive oil
2 tablespoons tomato purée
900 ml (1½ pints) brown rabbit
  stock
Sprigs of fresh coriander, to garnish

FOR THE MIREPOIX:
1 carrot, roughly chopped
½ an onion, chopped
1 celery stick, chopped
50 g (2 oz) celeriac, roughly diced
2 garlic cloves
5 green leek tops, sliced
1 sprig of fresh thyme
1 sprig of fresh rosemary

FOR THE DUMPLINGS:
175 g (6 oz) strong white flour
120 ml (4 fl oz) milk
15 g (½ oz) butter
7 g (¼ oz) fresh yeast
Pinch of sugar
Pinch of salt
2 tablespoons shredded suet
2–3 tablespoons chopped fresh
  parsley

FOR THE VEGETABLES:
1 swede
1 carrot
1 celeriac
1 courgette

Pre-heat the oven to 220°C/425°F/Gas 7.

Put the flour in a roasting tin and cook in the oven until slightly coloured, stirring occasionally. Leave to cool. Coat the rabbit pieces in the singed flour. Heat 4 tablespoons of oil in a flameproof casserole, add the rabbit pieces and fry until golden brown. Tip the rabbit pieces into a colander to remove the excess fat. Heat the remaining 2 tablespoons of oil in the casserole, add the vegetables and herbs for the mirepoix and cook for 2–3 minutes, taking care not to brown the vegetables. Add the rabbit pieces and tomato purée and cook for 2 minutes then add the rabbit stock. Bring to the boil, skim off any fat which has risen to the surface, then cover. Turn down the oven to 180°C/350°F/Gas 4 and cook for 1½ hours until tender.

Meanwhile, prepare the dumplings. Put the flour into the bowl of an electric mixer. Pour the milk into a pan, add the butter and bring to blood temperature. Put the yeast and sugar into a small bowl and mix to a smooth paste. Add the milk mixture and mix well together. Set the mixer to a low speed, pour the milk mixture onto the flour and mix for 5 minutes until firm and elastic. Add the salt and leave to stand for 12 minutes.

Turn the mixture onto a floured surface and knead for 2–3 minutes until smooth. Return to the bowl, cover and leave in a warm place for 30 minutes to rise.

Meanwhile, prepare and turn the vegetables by cutting into small, delicate shapes. Knead the dough again and allow to rise for another 30 minutes. Cook the turned vegetables in boiling salted water for 8–10 minutes until just crisp. Refresh in ice-cold water, drain and put to one side.

Knead the dough again for 2–3 minutes then leave to rise for a further 30 minutes. Knead the dough for a fourth time, then add the suet and chopped parsley, making sure it is well worked into the dough. Pinch off a small piece of dough, roll into a ball between the palms of your hands and place onto buttered greaseproof paper. Repeat with the remaining dough to make 15–20 balls. Cover and leave to rise for a further 2–3 minutes. When risen, steam the dumplings for about 3 minutes, remove and put on a plate.

Spoon the cooked rabbit pieces into a deep serving dish, cover and keep warm. Sieve the sauce, discarding the mirepoix, and, if necessary, boil the sauce to reduce it to the required consistency. Pour the sauce over the rabbit and add the cooked vegetables and dumplings. Serve garnished with coriander sprigs.

MEAT AND OFFAL

A high proportion of the British public is now more food-conscious than ever and, perhaps as a result of this, there has been a decline in the amount of red meat in our diet. The reasons for this are wide and varied and range from those of a humanitarian nature through to the scare created by B.S.E. (bovine spongiform encephalopathy, commonly known as mad cow disease) found in cattle. Even so, for some people, meat remains at the very heart of most meals and the range of recipes one has access to is vast. This chapter includes a selection of my favourite recipes and, given that I have scaled down the amount of meat I eat, I need to be sure that, when I do eat it, the dish will be extremely good.

Cooking meats is a very personal thing, so it's difficult to give prescriptive times for cooking particular joints. General guidelines include cooking pork thoroughly whilst leaving beef and lamb slightly undercooked.

When selecting beef look for lean meat with 'marbling'. This means there should be small flecks of fat inside the flesh and this keeps the meat moist during cooking.

Pork should have an even coating of soft white fat and the flesh should be springy to touch whilst lamb should have a thin coating of firm fat which mustn't be excessive and there should be evidence of 'marbling' running through the flesh.

Offal is a general term which covers a wide selection of edible parts of the animal which are not part of the main edible carcass. This includes the heart, kidneys, liver, sweetbreads (thymus and pancreas glands) brain, testicles and, in the case of beef, oxtail. If I were to be cast away on a desert island and could take only one prepared meal with me it would be braised oxtail. The reason? Simple – masses of flavour and it takes ages to eat!

Fillet of Beef with Wild Mushrooms and Mango

❦

This is a recipe put together following the abduction of a shopper in Surrey who had purchased a small fillet of beef and a mango. It was her intention to fry the fillet and use the mango as a vegetable to accompany the dish. Cooked together, they produce an astonishing amount of flavour and the mango gives moisture to what can often be a fairly dry meat.

Serves 6

750 g (1½ lb) beef fillet, trimmed
1 tablespoon walnut oil
175 g (6 oz) shallots, finely chopped
225 g (8 oz) assorted wild mushrooms
1 ripe mango, peeled, stoned and diced
1 bunch of fresh coriander, chopped

50 g (2 oz) dry breadcrumbs
2 plump tomatoes, skinned and chopped
4 tablespoons red wine (optional)
225 g (8 oz) puff pastry
1 egg, beaten
Salt and freshly ground black pepper

Pre-heat the oven to 200°C/400°F/Gas 6.

Heat the oil in a frying pan and add the beef. Season with salt and pepper and cook until sealed on all sides. Remove from the pan. Add the shallots and cook for 2–3 minutes until softened. Add the mushrooms, mango and coriander and cook for 1 minute. Then add the breadcrumbs, tomatoes and, if wished, the red wine. Season to taste with salt and pepper, then allow the mixture to cool.

On a lightly floured surface, roll out the pastry to a rectangle that will be large enough to wrap the fillet in. Place a layer of the filling mixture down the centre. Sit the beef fillet on top of the filling and cover with the remaining filling mixture. Brush the edges of the pastry with the beaten egg and fold the pastry over to enclose the beef. Seal the edges and turn the parcel over so that the join is underneath. Place on a baking tray.

Decorate the top of the pastry with a trellis of the reserved pastry and glaze all over with beaten egg. Leave to rest for at least 30 minutes. Bake for 20–25 minutes until golden brown.

Paupiettes of Beef

—— ❧❧❧ ——

Food that is cooked slowly in a liquid will often have far more taste than foods cooked by other methods. This dish has that, along with the added advantages of a tasty stuffing and a delicious sauce. It cries out for a serving of Almond Potatoes (see recipe on page 150).

Serves 4

750 g (1½ lb) topside of beef
175 g (6 oz) sausagemeat
1 tablespoon chopped fresh chervil
1 tablespoon chopped fresh tarragon
8 stoned black olives, chopped
2 tablespoons olive oil
50 g (2 oz) onion, chopped
50 g (2 oz) carrot, finely chopped
50 g (2 oz) leek, finely chopped

50 g (2 oz) celery, finely chopped
1 garlic clove, crushed
1 tablespoon tomato purée
3 tablespoons plain flour
175 ml (6 fl oz) red wine
900 ml (1½ pints) beef stock
1 bouquet garni
Salt and freshly ground black pepper

Pre-heat the oven to 150°C/300°F/Gas 2.

Trim the fat from the meat and cut the meat into 8 slices. Put the slices between sheets of greaseproof paper and beat with a wooden rolling pin or meat mallet until flat. Mix together the sausagemeat, chervil, tarragon and black olives. Spread the sausage mixture over each piece of meat, roll up and secure with string.

Heat the oil in a flameproof casserole, add the meat rolls and fry for 1–2 minutes to seal the meat. Remove from the casserole and put to one side. Add the chopped vegetables and garlic and cook for 5 minutes. Add the tomato purée and flour and mix together. Add the wine and stock and bring to the boil, stirring. Return the meat rolls to the casserole and add the bouquet garni. Season with salt and pepper.

Cook in the oven for 1½ hours until tender. Remove the paupiettes from the sauce, discard the string and place in a serving dish. Strain the sauce into a pan and, if necessary, boil to reduce the sauce to the required consistency. Check and, if necessary, adjust the seasoning. Pour the sauce over the meat and serve.

Beef Mediterranean

A nice simple dish, allowing the combination of ingredients to do all the work.
Serve with garlic bread.

Serves 4

1 tablespoon green peppercorns
1 tablespoon pink peppercorns
175 ml (6 fl oz) red wine
4 tablespoons sesame oil
450 g (1 lb) rump steak, thinly sliced into strips
1 garlic clove, crushed
1 tablespoon finely chopped fresh root ginger
1 tablespoon finely chopped fresh tarragon
1 tablespoon finely chopped fresh parsley
1 tablespoon snipped fresh chives

113-g (4-oz) can sliced bamboo shoots
50 g (2 oz) celery, sliced
50 g (2 oz) gherkins
100 g (4 oz) mushrooms, sliced
120 ml (4 fl oz) brandy
1 tablespoon tomato purée
225 g (8 oz) tomatoes, skinned, seeded and chopped
1 red pepper, seeded, cored and sliced
1 green pepper, seeded, cored and sliced
50 g (2 oz) mangetout
50 g (2 oz) baby sweetcorn
75 g (3 oz) broccoli

Soak the green and red peppercorns in the red wine for 15 minutes. Heat the oil in a flameproof casserole, add the meat and cook, stirring, until the meat is sealed. Add the garlic, ginger, chopped herbs, bamboo shoots, celery, gherkins and mushrooms. Add the brandy and burn off the alcohol by carefully tilting the casserole and setting alight. Stir well together. Add the peppercorns and red wine, tomato purée, tomatoes and peppers and stir gently. Finally, add the mangetout, sweetcorn and broccoli. Cover, turn to the lowest possible heat and simmer for about 25 minutes until tender.

Braised Beef studded with Ginger and Garlic

This dish is designed to bring together the freshness of the Orient and the traditional flavours synonymous with the best of British cookery. It was created from ingredients from a shopper's trolley, along with ingredients found in the same shopper's kitchen cupboard at home.

Serves 6

2 garlic cloves
25 g (1 oz) fresh root ginger
900 g (2 lb) silverside of beef
2 tablespoons vegetable oil
400-g (14-oz) can chopped tomatoes
200 g (7 oz) carrots, chopped
100 g (4 oz) celery, chopped

100 g (4 oz) leeks, sliced
250 g (9 oz) onions, chopped
2 tablespoons plain flour
300 ml (10 fl oz) beer
450 ml (15 fl oz) hot beef stock
Salt and freshly ground black pepper

Pre-heat the oven to 200°C/400°F/Gas 6.

Select a large casserole. Thinly slice the garlic cloves lengthways and cut the ginger into the same-sized pieces. Using a small, sharp knife, make deep incisions into the beef and insert a small piece of garlic and ginger into each incision. Season the meat with salt and pepper.

Heat the oil in a deep pan. Add the beef and cook for 2–3 minutes on all sides to seal. Remove from the pan and transfer to the casserole. Strain the tomatoes, reserving the juice. Put the carrots, celery, leeks and onions into the hot oil and cook for 2–3 minutes, stirring frequently. Add the chopped tomatoes then the flour and cook for 1 minute, stirring. Pour in the beer, tomato juice and the beef stock. Stir well and bring the sauce to the boil, stirring constantly. Season lightly with salt and pepper, then pour the sauce over the beef. Cover with a tight-fitting lid and cook in the oven for 1½ hours until the meat is tender.

Once cooked, remove the casserole from the oven and transfer the beef to a warmed serving dish. Cover and keep warm. Strain the sauce through a sieve or blend in a food processor. Pour into a pan and keep the sauce warm. Check and, if necessary, adjust the seasoning.

Carve the beef and pour the sauce over the slices before serving.

Beef Goulash

Spicy, but not hot, is how this Hungarian beef stew should be. I like to serve it with Paris-style Gnocchi (see recipe on page 62).

Serves 4

550 g (1¼ lb) topside beef, cubed
2 tablespoons paprika
2 tablespoons olive oil
225 g (8 oz) onions, chopped
2 garlic cloves, crushed
50 g (2 oz) plain flour

2 tablespoons tomato purée
600 ml (1 pint) beef stock
1 bouquet garni
100 g (4 oz) potatoes, diced
Salt and freshly ground black pepper

Pre-heat the oven to 180°C/350°F/Gas 4.

Roll the meat in the paprika. Heat the oil in a flameproof casserole. Add the meat and cook, stirring, until the meat is sealed on all sides but not browned. Add the onions and garlic and cook for a further 2 minutes, then dust with the flour and mix together. Add the tomato purée and beef stock and bring to the boil, stirring. Add the bouquet garni and season with salt and pepper.

Cover and bake in the oven for 1¼ hours. Add the potatoes and bake for a further 20 minutes until the potatoes are tender. Check and, if necessary, adjust the seasoning and the consistency. If it's too thick add a little more stock (or red wine) or if it's too thin then boil on the stove for 2–3 minutes to reduce the liquid, but be sure not to let the ingredients burn to the bottom of the pan.

Steak Tartare

— ❧❀❧ —

Not one for the faint-hearted! This classical dish is really eaten as described.
Serve with a crisp dressed salad.

For one serving

100 g (4 oz) fillet of beef
A selection of your favourite ingre-
dients, such as anchovies, capers,
garlic, shallots, fresh herbs

1 egg yolk
Salt and freshly ground black pepper

Remove any sinew from the beef, then mince or finely chop the meat. Shape the
beef into a thick disc and create a hollow in the centre. Finely chop your selected
ingredients then mix with the egg yolk and season with salt and pepper. Place
the mixture in the hollow and serve.

Carbonnade of Beef

— ❧❀❧ —

This very earthy dish has no frills whatsoever. It is what it is. An accompaniment of lightly buttered spinach and Biarritz Potatoes (see recipe on page 151)
complete the picture.

Serves 4

750 g (1½ lb) topside of beef, cut
into 8 steaks
1 teaspoon crushed black pepper-
corns
1 tablespoon olive oil
225 g (8 oz) onions, sliced

1 tablespoon chopped fresh tarragon
2 garlic cloves, crushed
1 tablespoon plain flour
300 ml (10 fl oz) brown ale
1 bay leaf
Salt

Pre-heat the oven to 150°C/300°F/Gas 2.
Season the steaks with salt and the crushed peppercorns. Heat the oil in a

large flameproof casserole, add the steaks and cook until browned on both sides. Remove from the casserole and put to one side. Add the onions, tarragon and garlic and cook, stirring, for about 5 minutes until the onions have become dark brown. Add the flour and cook for 1 minute, stirring. Pour in the ale and bring to the boil, stirring. Return the steaks to the casserole and add the bay leaf. Cover and cook in the oven for 2 hours until the meat is tender. Remove the bay leaf before serving.

Forfar Bridies

This dish came about following an encounter with a Scottish lady living in Kent with a hankering for mince and tatties. She explained that, as funds were low, she needed a dish that was inexpensive yet tasty and one that would leave the family feeling loved and full. Hence the tatties (Scottish for potatoes, in case you didn't already know). This recipe is more interesting, just as filling and no more expensive than the traditional dish.

Makes 4

2 tablespoons olive oil
100 g (4 oz) onions, finely chopped
50 g (2 oz) carrot, finely chopped
50 g (2 oz) leek, finely chopped
1 tablespoon chopped fresh parsley
Pinch of ground ginger

225 g (8 oz) minced beef
4 tablespoons beef stock
350 g (12 oz) puff pastry
1 egg, lightly beaten
Salt and freshly ground black pepper

Heat the oil in a pan, add the onions, carrot, leek, parsley and ginger and cook gently for 5 minutes until softened. Add the minced beef and stock, season with salt and pepper and mix together.

Pre-heat the oven to 180°C/350°F/Gas 4.

On a lightly floured surface, roll out the pastry and cut into 4 rounds the size of an individual plate or a large saucer. Place a portion of the meat mixture on one side of the pastry rounds. Wet the edges with a little water and fold over. Using a fork, prick the centre and brush with the beaten egg. Place on a baking tray and bake for 20–25 minutes until golden brown. Serve hot.

Fillet of Lamb rubbed in Fresh Herbs and baked in a Salt Crust

The credit for this dish goes to John Burton Race at L'Ortolan in Shinfield. The aroma from the lamb when the pastry is cut open is memorable. I know it's obvious, but don't eat the pastry!

Serves 6

5 tablespoons olive oil
2 best ends of lamb, total weight about 2.25 kg (5 lb), filleted, with bones chopped for stock
1 onion, chopped
½ a carrot, chopped
1 celery stick, chopped
1 small leek, chopped
6 ripe tomatoes
25 g (1 oz) tomato purée
1 sprig of fresh thyme
4 garlic cloves, crushed
1.5 litres (2½ pints) chicken stock
1 tablespoon Dijon mustard
Beaten egg, to glaze
Freshly ground black pepper

FOR THE SALT CRUST:
200 g (7 oz) plain white flour
175 g (6 oz) coarse sea salt

Leaves from 1 sprig of fresh thyme, finely chopped
Leaves from 1 sprig of fresh rosemary, finely chopped
1 egg, size 6, and 1 yolk

FOR THE GARNISH:
8 garlic cloves
20 shallots
Pinch of caster sugar
50 g (2 oz) butter
1 teaspoon lemon juice
Salt and freshly ground black pepper

FOR THE PARSLEY CRUSTS:
150 g (5 oz) fresh white breadcrumbs
90 g (3½ oz) chopped fresh parsley
1 garlic clove, crushed
½ a bay leaf
Leaves from 1 sprig of fresh thyme
Olive oil, to bind

Pre-heat the oven to 220°C/425°F/Gas 7.

Heat 3 tablespoons of the oil in a flameproof casserole. Carefully add the chopped bones without splashing the oil, then roast in the oven for 30–40 minutes, turning occasionally until evenly browned. Remove the bones with a slotted spoon and reserve. Return the oil to the stove and carefully add the vegetables except the tomatoes. Fry until browned but with no black pieces as this can make the stock bitter. Remove the vegetables with a slotted spoon and reserve. Squeeze the whole tomatoes into the pan, also adding the flesh. Add the tomato purée, thyme, garlic, reserved bones and vegetables and cover with the chicken stock. Bring to the boil, skim off any scum and simmer for 1 hour.

Meanwhile, prepare the salt crust. Sift the flour into a bowl and add the sea salt, thyme, rosemary leaves, egg and egg yolk. Work together in a machine or by hand for 5 minutes. The dough should be firm and pliable. If it is too wet add a little flour, too dry add a few drops of water. On no account should the dough be too wet. Form the dough into a ball, wrap in cling film and leave for at least 30 minutes to relax and for the herbs to permeate through the dough.

To prepare the garnish, cut any large garlic clove in half lengthways and put in a pan. Cover with cold water and bring to the boil. When boiling, strain, cover with cold water and bring to the boil again. (This helps to make the garlic more mild in flavour.) On the final boil cook until the cloves are tender then strain and put to one side.

In a shallow pan, large enough to hold all the shallots sitting on top of each other, put in the shallots, sugar, a pinch of salt, pepper, butter, lemon juice and enough water to come two-thirds up the sides of the shallots. Bring to the boil, cover with buttered greaseproof paper and cook slowly for 5 minutes. Remove the paper and check on the cooking stage. If nearly cooked, remove the paper and increase the heat to boil off all the remaining liquid. This should take 2 minutes and the shallots should be tender and glistening. Put to one side.

To prepare the parsley crusts, blend the breadcrumbs and parsley together in a food processor. Add the crushed garlic. Chop or crush the bay leaf in a pestle and mortar. Add the breadcrumbs with the thyme and mix well together. Season with salt and pepper. Whilst the machine is running, slowly add a little olive oil until the breadcrumbs begin to bind together but keep loose. The mixture should be moist and crumbly. Check and adjust the seasoning if necessary.

Season the lamb fillets with pepper only. Heat the remaining 2 tablespoons of oil in a frying pan and fry the fillets until sealed all over, including the ends. Drain on kitchen paper and dry thoroughly.

Roll out the salt crust into 2 x 1-cm (½-in) thick rectangles. Spread the lamb fillets with mustard and roll in the parsley crust mixture. Place a fillet in the centre of each rectangle and roll up, completely covering the fillets with the salt crust. Trim the ends and tuck under any excess crust. Leave no holes. Brush generously with beaten egg and bake in the oven for only 10 minutes until golden brown.

Strain off the stock, skim, return to the boil and reduce to one-third. Season with salt and pepper to taste. Strain through a muslin cloth to produce a clear stock.

In a hot roasting tin, add the blanched garlic cloves and the shallots and roast for 10 minutes until golden brown. Season with salt and pepper. Place the cooked lamb on a board with the shallots and garlic. Pour the sauce into a jug or a sauce boat. To serve, break open the crusts, lift out the fillets, slice and garnish with the shallots and garlic. Spoon over the sauce.

Lamb Cutlets baked with a Rice and Onion Crust

❦

The rice and onion topping for these cutlets can be made well in advance and even frozen. It adds a different dimension to the dish and does, in fact, produce an abundance of compliments for very little effort.

Serves 4

12 lamb cutlets	A sprig of fresh thyme
50 g (2 oz) butter	1 teaspoon curry powder
75 g (3 oz) onion, chopped	2 egg yolks
100 g (4 oz) long-grain rice	50 ml (2 fl oz) double cream
450 ml (15 fl oz) chicken stock	Salt and freshly ground black pepper
1 bay leaf	4 sprigs of fresh rosemary, to garnish

Season the lamb cutlets with salt and pepper. Heat the butter in a large frying pan, add the cutlets and cook on both sides until sealed. Transfer to a large baking tray and put to one side. Pour the fat from the frying pan into a deep pan and heat. Add the onion and cook for 1 minute without browning. Pour in the rice and cook for a further 2 minutes, stirring continuously.

Add the stock, bay leaf and thyme and season with salt and pepper. Bring to boil, then reduce the heat and simmer for 15 minutes until the stock has been absorbed and the rice is tender. Remove from the heat and leave to cool.

Pre-heat the oven to 220°C/425°F/Gas 7. Blend the rice mixture in a food processor until smooth. Add the curry powder and egg yolks. Mix well together. Slowly add the cream, being careful not to curdle the mixture, and mix until it reaches a consistency suitable for piping. Place the mixture into a piping bag fitted with a large star nozzle and pipe the mixture on top of the cutlets. Bake for 10–12 minutes until golden brown. Serve garnished with a sprig of fresh rosemary.

Navarin of Lamb

※

This is a complete meal and requires only a bottle of red wine and some good company with perhaps a roaring fire on a cold winter's day to make it a memorable meal. It's even nicer when re-heated the following day. If you have difficulty in getting neck of lamb then ask your butcher for breast, but be sure to remove all the fat.

Serves 4

750 g (1½ lb) best end neck of lamb, cut into single rib pieces
25 g (1 oz) dripping
50 g (2 oz) onion, chopped
50 g (2 oz) celery, chopped
50 g (2 oz) carrot, chopped
50 g (2 oz) leek, chopped
1 garlic clove, crushed
½ teaspoon crushed black pepper-corns
50 g (2 oz) plain flour
40 g (1½ oz) tomato purée
175 ml (6 fl oz) red wine

600 ml (1 pint) beef stock
1 bouquet garni
100 g (4 oz) button onions
100 g (4 oz) carrots, cut into thin 5-mm (¼-in) fingers
100 g (4 oz) celery, peeled and cut into thin 5-mm (¼-in) fingers
100 g (4 oz) turnips, peeled and cut into thin 5-mm (¼-in) fingers
100 g (4 oz) button mushrooms
100 g (4 oz) potatoes, cut into thin 5-mm (¼-in) fingers
Salt and freshly ground black pepper

Pre-heat the oven to 180°C/350°F/Gas 4.

Heat the dripping in a flameproof casserole, add the meat and season with salt and pepper. Cook for 5 minutes, turning the meat continuously, ensuring it is evenly sealed and browned. Add the chopped onion, celery, carrot, leek, garlic and crushed peppercorns. Mix together and cook for a further 3 minutes. Cook in the oven for 10 minutes. Remove from the oven and mix the flour into the ingredients. Add the tomato purée and red wine then gradually stir in the stock. Bring slowly to the boil, stirring, then add the bouquet garni. Cover and return to the oven and cook for a further 1½ hours. Add the button onions, neatly cut vegetable fingers, mushrooms and potatoes. Return to the oven and cook for a further 20 minutes until the meat and vegetables are tender. Season with salt and pepper and serve.

Salad of Southdown Lamb in Mustard and Spices with Mushrooms cooked in Honey

❧✦❧

Lamb from any part of the country will work in this recipe. It just so happens that during filming we acquired Southdown lamb.

Serves 4

1 boned loin of lamb (from best end of neck), about 450 g (1 lb)
Dijon mustard
1 tablespoon wholegrain mustard
1 teaspoon ground cumin
1 teaspoon ground coriander
½ tablespoon ground ginger
1 teaspoon garlic powder
25 g (1 oz) butter
90 g (3½ oz) mixed wild mushrooms, chopped

50 g (2 oz) shallots, finely chopped
2 tablespoons clear honey
2 tomatoes, skinned and finely chopped
Dressed salad leaves
2 tablespoons snipped fresh chives
2 tablespoons chopped fresh chervil
2 tablespoons chopped fresh tarragon
2 tablespoons chopped fresh dill
Salt and freshly ground black pepper

Pre-heat the oven to 180°C/350°F/Gas 4.

Season the lamb with salt and pepper then spread with the Dijon and wholegrain mustard. Roll up the meat and tie at intervals. Mix together the cumin, coriander, ginger and garlic powder, and dip the meat in the spices. Place the meat in a hot flameproof casserole and fry the meat in its own fat for about 2 minutes until sealed on all sides and lightly browned. Transfer to the oven and cook for 12–15 minutes until tender.

Meanwhile, heat the butter in a pan, add the mushrooms and shallots and fry for 5 minutes until softened. Pour on the honey. Push the mushrooms to one side of the pan then add the tomatoes and season with salt and pepper. Mix together the salad leaves and herbs, and arrange in the centre of the plates. Cut the lamb into slices and place around the salad. Spoon the mushrooms and their juice around the lamb and serve.

Sweet and Sour Pork

❦❦❦

An authentic Chinese recipe following very classical lines which was cooked for a person in Southampton who had never eaten Chinese food.
His reaction? Fabulous!

Serves 4

350 g (12 oz) pork tenderloin, sliced
1 tablespoon dry sherry
2 tablespoons soy sauce
1 egg, lightly beaten
3 tablespoons cornflour
Oil, for deep frying
150 ml (5 fl oz) chicken stock
2 tablespoons tarragon vinegar
1 tablespoon brown sugar

1 tablespoon tomato purée
1 tablespoon cold water
50 g (2 oz) spring onions, chopped
75 g (3 oz) green pepper, seeded and chopped
75 g (3 oz) red pepper, seeded and chopped
50 g (2 oz) carrot, finely chopped
1 orange, segmented
Salt and freshly ground black pepper

Put the meat into a large bowl with the sherry and 1 tablespoon of the soy sauce. Season with salt and pepper and leave in the refrigerator to marinate for 2 hours.

Mix together the egg and 2 tablespoons of the cornflour and beat until smooth. Drain the pieces of pork and dip each piece into the batter. Heat the oil for frying to 180°C/350°F, then deep-fry the pork pieces for 5–8 minutes until golden brown. Drain on kitchen paper.

Meanwhile, mix together the chicken stock, the remaining soy sauce, tarragon vinegar, sugar and tomato purée in a pan and bring to the boil. Blend the remaining 1 tablespoon of cornflour with the water and then whisk it into liquid. Remove from the heat. Season with a little salt. Add the spring onions, peppers and carrot and heat gently. Add the orange segments and cooked pork and serve.

Stuffed Loin of Pork on a bed of Lentils with Caramelized Apples

❧❦❧

This recipe produces a really delicious, moist dish and transforms a relatively plain, albeit tasty, joint of meat into a much more interesting one. Do feel free to experiment with the herbs. The nice thing about pork is that it plays a willing host to most flavours.

Serves 4

4 boneless loin of pork chops, about 100 g (4 oz) each
100 g (4 oz) lean raw ham
1 egg yolk
120 ml (4 fl oz) double cream
Pinch of cayenne pepper
1 tablespoon snipped fresh chives
½ tablespoon vegetable oil
50 g (2 oz) smoked streaky bacon, rind removed and diced
50 g (2 oz) carrot, chopped
1 medium onion, chopped
50 g (2 oz) celery, chopped

75 g (3 oz) brown Puy lentils, washed and drained
450 ml (15 fl oz) chicken stock
1 tablespoon chopped fresh oregano
50 g (2 oz) butter
120 ml (4 fl oz) dry cider
75 g (3 oz) chilled butter, cut into small pieces
2 large eating apples
75 g (3 oz) demerara sugar
Salt and freshly ground black pepper
8 chervil leaves, to garnish

Pre-heat the oven to 180°C/350°F/Gas 4.

Slice the pork chops lengthways, almost to the bottom, and open out. Place each piece between sheets of greaseproof paper and, using a wooden rolling pin, beat until flattened. Mince the raw ham in a food processor, add the egg yolk and blend for 1 minute. Add the cream and mix until slightly thick. Season with cayenne, salt and pepper and mix in the chives. Place the mixture into a refrigerator to chill for at least 30 minutes.

Heat the oil in a heavy-based flameproof casserole. Add the bacon and cook for 4 minutes. Add the vegetables and cook for a further 5 minutes, stirring frequently. Add the lentils, stock, oregano and season with salt and pepper. Bring to the boil, then cover. Cook for 40–45 minutes until tender, stirring occasionally and adding more stock during cooking if necessary. Check and, if necessary, adjust the seasoning.

Spread the chilled ham mixture evenly over the pork steaks. Roll them up like a Swiss roll and secure with either string or cocktail sticks. Heat the butter in a flameproof casserole, add the pork rolls and cook until sealed and just lightly browned. Add the cider and cover. Cook in the oven for 30–40 minutes until tender. Remove the pork rolls from the liquid and keep warm. Place the casserole on a high heat, bring to the boil and boil until reduced to one-third. Remove from the heat and gently shake the pan whilst adding the chilled pieces of butter. Do not reheat the sauce. Core and cut the apples into thick slices. Cover the apple slices with the sugar and caramelize either under the grill or in the oven. Put the lentil mixture into 4 dariole or ramekin dishes and turn out onto large plates. Remove the string from the pork, slice each piece of meat into 4 thick rounds and place around the lentil puddings. Place the apples to the side of the meat and surround with the sauce. Garnish with the chervil and serve.

Chump Chop Champvallon

This is a real winner on a bleak midwinter's evening when all the family have had a hard day at work or school and arrive home wet and tired. Do select chops which have a minimal amount of fat or, if necessary, remove any surplus.

Serves 4

4 large (100 g/4 oz) or 8 small
  (50 g/2 oz) chump chops
2 tablespoons olive oil
2 sprigs of fresh rosemary
1 large onion, sliced
4 tomatoes, skinned and sliced

4 medium potatoes, sliced
4 tablespoons sherry
350 ml (12 fl oz) chicken stock
75 g (3 oz) butter, melted
Salt and freshly ground black pepper

Season the chops with salt and pepper. Heat the oil in a frying pan and cook the chops until sealed on both sides but not browned. Place the chops in a deep casserole and add the rosemary. Layer with onion, then tomatoes and finally with potatoes, seasoning each layer with salt and pepper. Pour over the sherry and chicken stock and brush the top with melted butter. Cook in the oven for 1–1¼ hours until the potatoes are cooked, crisp and golden brown.

Spiked, Glazed Gammon

— ❧❀❧ —

I often cook this when friends are coming round for a drink. It looks lovely when placed on the table before your guests. Serve with lots of warm French bread and pickles. The left-overs taste just as good the following day.

Serves 6

1.5 kg (3½ lb) gammon joint
2 carrots
1 small onion
2 celery sticks

1 bay leaf
Dijon mustard
24 cloves
75 g (3 oz) demerara sugar

Put the gammon in a large pan, add the vegetables and bay leaf and cover with cold water. Bring to the boil and pour off the water. Rinse the vegetables and gammon in cold water. Cover again with fresh cold water, bring to the boil and simmer for 1 hour.

Pre-heat the oven to 200°C/400°F/Gas 6.

Remove the gammon from the liquid. Using a sharp knife, strip the skin off the gammon. Score the surface of the fat to create a diamond effect, smother with mustard, press a clove into the centre of each diamond and cover the whole joint with the sugar. Bake for 30–50 minutes until tender. Serve hot or cold.

Braised Oxtail

✻

Of all the dishes based upon slow-cooked meat this is my favourite. Oxtail is very meaty and gives its cooking liquid the most superb flavour and aroma. This is a dish which demands to be picked up and eaten using the fingers, and I recall many happy meals drawing the last drops of flavour from the bone.

It is always a good idea to serve it with a small bowl of warm water and a serviette so you and your guests can clean up after the meal! I usually keep back a little of the sauce for the following day and serve myself a large bowl of oxtail soup just by re-heating it.

Serves 4

25 ml (1 fl oz) sunflower oil
1.25 kg (2½ lb) oxtail, chopped
100 g (4 oz) carrots, chopped
100 g (4 oz) onions, chopped
100 g (4 oz) leeks, sliced
100 g (4 oz) celery, chopped
50 g (2 oz) plain flour
50 g (2 oz) tomato purée

1.25 litres (2¼ pints) hot beef stock
1 bouquet garni
Salt and freshly ground black pepper
Selection of freshly boiled vegetables, to serve

Pre-heat the oven to 200°C/400°F/Gas 6. Heat the oil in a large, flame-proof casserole dish, add the oxtail and cook to seal on both sides. Using a slotted spoon, remove from the pan. Add the chopped vegetables to the hot oil and cook for 5–6 minutes, stirring constantly. Add the flour and mix thoroughly into the oil and vegetables, ensuring all of the oil has been absorbed into the flour. Continue cooking for 3–4 minutes, then mix in the tomato purée. Gradually pour in the stock, stirring constantly, then return the oxtail to the sauce. Add the bouquet garni, season with salt and pepper to taste and cover tightly.

Cook in the oven for 2½–3 hours. To serve, simply add some freshly boiled vegetables of your choice, to put some fresh colour into the dish.

Stuffed Lambs' Hearts

To my mind, hearts are one of the tastiest ingredients available to cooks. Granted, they are not the easiest of foods to prepare, but for a little effort the reward is high.

Serves 2

2 lambs' hearts

FOR THE STUFFING:
15 g (½ oz) butter
25 g (1 oz) shallots, finely chopped
25 g (1 oz) mushrooms, finely chopped
1 tablespoon chopped mixed fresh herbs
　　such as rosemary, thyme, parsley
25 g (1 oz) fresh breadcrumbs
100 g (4 oz) sausagemeat

FOR THE SAUCE:
50 g (2 oz) butter
1 rasher of bacon
50 g (2 oz) carrot, roughly chopped

50 g (2 oz) celery, roughly chopped
50 g (2 oz) leek, roughly chopped
50 g (2 oz) shallots, roughly chopped
1 garlic clove, finely chopped
50 g (2 oz) plain flour
25 g (1 oz) tomato purée
1.2 litres (2 pints) brown stock
150 ml (5 fl oz) red wine

FOR THE GARNISH:
100 g (4 oz) cabbage, sliced
2 carrots, cut into small, delicate shapes
6 shallots
25 g (1 oz) butter
Salt and freshly ground black pepper

Cut the hearts down one side to open out and remove the tubes. Wash well and pat dry.

To make the stuffing, heat the butter in a pan, add the shallots and mushrooms and cook until softened. Add the chopped herbs. Remove from the heat and stir in the breadcrumbs. Leave to cool then add the sausagemeat and mix together. Use the stuffing to fill the hearts. Using a trussing needle, sew up the hearts with fine string, then wrap in muslin.

Heat the butter for the sauce in a pan, add the hearts and cook until sealed on all sides. Transfer to a casserole dish. Add the bacon to the pan and fry until the fat starts to run then transfer to the casserole dish. Add the carrot, celery, leek, shallots and garlic to the pan and fry for 5 minutes. Then add the flour and cook, stirring constantly, until the mixture browns slightly. Add the tomato purée. Gradually add the brown stock and the red wine, stirring continuously. Simmer for 30 minutes.

Pre-heat the oven to 180°C/350°F/Gas 4.

Pour the sauce over the hearts and cook in the oven for about 1½ hours until tender. Just before serving, prepare the garnish. Cook the cabbage, carrots and shallots in a pan of salted water for 5 minutes until tender. Toss lightly in the butter and check and adjust the seasoning if necessary.

Remove the hearts from the casserole and remove the muslin and string. Place the hearts on warmed serving plates and strain over the sauce. Garnish with the vegetables and serve.

Lambs' Kidneys in a Mustard Sauce

The big mistake here is to overcook the kidneys. They toughen
if they are cooked too much.

Serves 4

100 g (4 oz) butter
900 g (2 lb) lambs' kidneys, skinned,
   cored and halved
100 g (4 oz) shallots, finely chopped
50 g (2 oz) celery, finely chopped
1 garlic clove, crushed

½ teaspoon crushed black peppercorns
300 ml (10 fl oz) dry white wine
2 tablespoons Meaux mustard
Salt and freshly ground black pepper
1 tablespoon chopped fresh chervil,
   to garnish

Melt 50 g (2 oz) of the butter in a frying pan, add the kidneys and season with salt and pepper. Cook for 5–8 minutes until tender. Remove from the pan and place in a warmed serving dish.

Add the shallots, celery, garlic and crushed peppercorns to the pan and cook for 5 minutes. Pour in the wine then boil until reduced by half. Gradually whisk in the remaining 50 g (2 oz) butter. Add the mustard and season with salt and pepper to taste. Strain the sauce over the kidneys and serve garnished with the chervil.

Hungarian-style Lambs' Liver

Any reference to Hungarian, from a cookery point of view, refers to the use of paprika, and is particularly suitable with liver.

Serves 4

100 g (4 oz) butter
100 g (4 oz) onions, sliced
1 large green pepper
450 g (1 lb) lambs' liver, thinly sliced
75 g (3 oz) plain flour
1 tablespoon paprika

150 ml (5 fl oz) white wine
150 ml (5 fl oz) double cream
Juice of 1 lemon
Salt and freshly ground black pepper
3 tomatoes, skinned, seeded and diced

Seed and thinly slice the green pepper. Melt 50 g (2 oz) of the butter in a frying pan, add the onions and green pepper and cook gently for 5 minutes without browning. Remove from the pan and put aside. Coat the liver with flour and shake off excess. Melt the remaining butter in the pan and add the liver. Season with salt and pepper and cook for 1 minute. Add the onions and pepper. Turn the liver, add the paprika and white wine and boil until reduced by half. Pour in the cream and add the lemon juice. Remove from the heat. Place the liver, with the onions and the pepper, on warmed serving plates and pour over the sauce. Garnish with a heaped teaspoon of tomato flesh on the top.

Sausage and Capsicum Bake

Economical and full of flavour, this dish is perfect for a large family.

Serves 4

8 sausages (use your favourite type)
2 tablespoons olive oil
2 green peppers, seeded and sliced
1 red pepper, seeded and sliced
1 small onion, peeled and sliced

450 g (1 lb) potatoes
300 ml (½ pint) chicken stock or
   red wine
50 g (2 oz) butter, melted
Salt and freshly ground black pepper

Pre-heat the oven to 190°C/375°F/Gas 5.

Cut the sausages in half. Heat the oil in a pan, add the sliced peppers and onions and cook gently for 5 minutes, without colouring. Transfer the vegetables to a casserole dish and lay the sausage over the top. Peel and slice the potatoes and lay over the sausages. Add the chicken stock or wine and season with salt and pepper. Brush the surface of the potatoes with the melted butter and cook in the oven for 1 hour until golden brown.

Sausage Pilaff

⋅⊰⊱⋅

This recipe was created for an angel (6 years old from Canterbury) who was going through that difficult 'I'm not eating that' stage. I have to admit that it's become one of my favourites, but then I am a sausage freak. The dish is further enhanced by carefully flaking a little butter onto the pilaff before serving.

Serves 4

50 g (2 oz) butter
50 g (2 oz) onion, chopped
2 tablespoons chopped fresh tarragon
2 tablespoons chopped fresh parsley
50 g (2 oz) streaky bacon
150 g (5 oz) basmati rice
75 g (3 oz) mushrooms, chopped
100 g (4 oz) tomatoes, skinned,
    seeded and chopped

113-g (4-oz) can sweetcorn
50 g (2 oz) cashew nuts
450 g (1 lb) pork sausages, sliced
    into chunks
450 ml (15 fl oz) chicken or
    vegetable stock
Salt and freshly ground black pepper
Sprigs of fresh herbs, to garnish

In a large casserole or pan, heat the butter then add the onions, herbs, bacon and the rice. Mix well and cook for 30 seconds. Add all the remaining ingredients, leaving the sausages and stock until last. Season well with salt and pepper.

Cover the ingredients with greaseproof paper to seal in the flavour, then place a lid on the pan and simmer for 20 minutes until the rice has absorbed all the liquid and the vegetables are tender. Check and, if necessary, adjust the seasoning. Garnish with fresh herbs and serve immediately.

VEGETABLES

It's a sad fact of life, but too many people, especially professional chefs, pay too little attention to vegetables and potatoes. The fact of the matter is that they actually form at least 50 per cent of a conventional British main course. If the main dish is spectacular, but the vegetables and potatoes are awful, the whole meal is a disaster.

Once again, supermarkets are to be commended for the range and quality of vegetables that they make available to the public. It's also a good idea to use Asian/Afro-Caribbean shops (providing they are within easy reach) for herbs and vegetables as they often have ample supplies of unusual items which can be considerably cheaper than in the larger supermarkets.

Vegetables need to be purchased as and when you require them as they deteriorate very quickly. Bulk buying therefore is not such a good idea, although potatoes are the exception to this rule.

The recipes I've included here are just some of my favourite vegetable recipes and will do credit to your main dish.

Vegetables are an important element in our lives. They provide us with many of the vitamins and nutrients that our body needs to survive and they present themselves as an economical addition to our daily diet.

These days the selection of fresh vegetables from all parts of the world is better than it has ever been. The British shopper is no longer faced with the choice of carrots or sprouts as the only quality vegetables available in the local supermarket. There are now pumpkin, artickoke, chard, asparagus, okra, kohl rabi... the list goes on. But even with this choice we still need to prepare and cook them in such a way so as to retain colour, flavour and goodness. I always feel we don't pay enough consideration to the choice and cooking technique of vegetables. So, where possible try boiling in stock rather than boiling in plain water, steaming if the vegetable is delicate in texture and flavours and roasting if it is robust. The flavour is enhanced if you season during the cooking stage.

Pumpkin cooked with a Tomato and Black Olive Sauce

This much underused vegetable is highly adaptable and willing to take on new flavours by adding other ingredients. It's also relatively inexpensive.

Serves 4

750 g (1½ lb) pumpkin
100 g (4 oz) unsalted butter
100 g (4 oz) onions, sliced
2 garlic cloves, crushed
3 tablespoons chopped fresh basil
1 tablespoon chopped fresh coriander
1 teaspoon finely ground black pepper
50 g (2 oz) girolle mushrooms, sliced
50 ml (2 fl oz) olive oil

8 large tomatoes, skinned, seeded and chopped
1 tablespoon tomato purée
50 g (2 oz) stoned black olives, halved
3 drops of Tabasco sauce
1 teaspoon Worcestershire sauce
Pinch of sugar
Salt and freshly ground black pepper

Skin the pumpkin and remove the seeds. Cut the flesh into small cubes. Heat the butter in a wide pan, add the onions, garlic and herbs, and cook for 2–3 minutes until soft. Add the pepper and mushrooms and cook for a further 1 minute.

In a separate pan, heat the oil, add the pumpkin and tomatoes, season with salt and pepper and cook for a further 1 minute. Mix in the tomato purée and olives and combine this mixture with the ingredients in the first pan. Season with Tabasco, Worcestershire sauce and a pinch of sugar. Mix together and serve hot.

Creamed Beetroot

❦

This recipe came about after my encounter with a shopper who had selected a jar of beetroot to serve with a salad. Following our cookery session he agreed that there is no comparison between a jar of beetroot and fresh beetroot.

Serves 4

750 g (1½ lb) fresh raw beetroots
300 ml (10 fl oz) double cream
2 tablespoons chopped fresh coriander

Juice of ½ a lemon
75 g (3 oz) unsalted butter
Salt and freshly ground black pepper

Peel the beetroots and cut the flesh into 5-mm (¼-in) dice. Cook in a little boiling salted water for 10–15 minutes until tender. Drain, cover and keep warm.

Put the cream in a heavy-based pan and, stirring frequently, bring to the boil. Cook until reduced by half then add the chopped coriander and lemon juice. Remove from the heat, then whisk in the butter. Season with salt and pepper to taste. Pour the sauce over the beetroot and serve hot.

Parsnips in a Turmeric Cream Sauce

❦

Parsnips are, to my mind, one of the most underrated vegetables in existence. Presented in this manner they will enhance any meal.

Serves 4

750g (1½ lb) parsnips
Juice of ½ a lemon
25 g (1 oz) butter
25 g (1 oz) shallots, finely chopped

1 tablespoon turmeric
120 ml (4 fl oz) dry vermouth
275 ml (9 fl oz) cream
Salt and freshly ground black pepper

Peel and cut the parsnips into thick matchsticks. Put in a pan of salted water and add the lemon juice. Cook for 10 minutes until tender. Drain well and pat dry.

Heat the butter in a pan, add the shallots and turmeric and cook for 2 minutes. Add the parsnips and season with salt and pepper. Pour in the vermouth and boil until reduced by half. Add the cream, mix together and heat through before serving. Check and adjust the seasoning if necessary.

Stuffed Aubergines

Aubergine is such a versatile vegetable and, prepared in this manner, it makes a lovely accompaniment to a really meaty main course or could quite easily be served on its own as a snack.

Serves 4

2 aubergines
6 tablespoons olive oil
50 g (2 oz) shallots, finely chopped
175 g (6 oz) mushrooms, finely chopped
175 g (6 oz) tomatoes, chopped

1 tablespoon chopped fresh basil
50 g (2 oz) fresh breadcrumbs
25 g (1 oz) Parmesan, freshly grated
2 tablespoons chopped fresh parsley
Salt and freshly ground black pepper

Pre-heat the oven to 180°C/350°F/Gas 4.

Cut the stalks off the aubergines, then cut them in half lengthways. Score the centre of the aubergine flesh criss-cross and brush well with about 4 tablespoons of the oil. Bake for 15 minutes until tender. Scoop out and finely chop the aubergine flesh. Reserve the shells.

Heat the remaining 2 tablespoons of olive oil in a pan, add the shallots and cook gently for 2–3 minutes until soft. Add the mushrooms, tomatoes, aubergine and the basil, and season with salt and pepper. Cook for 5 minutes then transfer the mixture into the empty aubergine shells.

Mix together the breadcrumbs, Parmesan and parsley and sprinkle over the aubergines. Cook under a hot grill until golden brown.

Ratatouille Niçoise

❦

A vegetables chapter would be incomplete without this recipe.
It is particularly good served with chicken.

Serves 4

2 large aubergines
3 large courgettes
4 tablespoons olive oil
1 large onion, chopped
3 garlic cloves, crushed
2 red peppers, seeded and chopped
2 green peppers, seeded and chopped

175 ml (6 fl oz) white wine
  (optional)
4 tablespoons chopped fresh basil
6 large tomatoes, skinned, seeded
  and chopped
Salt and freshly ground black pepper

Cut the aubergines in half lengthways then cut them into 2.5-cm (1-in) slices. Cut the courgettes into 2.5-cm (1-in) slices. Place the aubergines and courgettes on a tray and sprinkle with salt. Cover with a clean cloth and place a heavy object such as a chopping board on top. Leave to stand for 30 minutes.

Heat the oil in a wide-based pan, add the onion and garlic, and cook for 5 minutes. Rinse then dry the aubergines and courgettes on kitchen paper and then add to the pan. Add the red and green peppers and cook for 5 minutes, then add the wine, basil and tomatoes. Season with salt and pepper, cover and cook gently for 15 minutes until the vegetables are tender.

RIGHT: *Biarritz Potatoes*
OVERLEAF: *Gnocchi Romaine* and *Tortelloni in a Tuna and Lemon Dressing*
PAGES 140–144: *Pumpkin cooked with a Tomato and Black Olive Sauce* and *Parkin;*
Lemon and Pistachio Soufflé and *Warm Lemon Tart;*
Oeufs à la Neige

Byron Potatoes

This dish was described by the lady who cooked it with me as 'a really wicked dish'. If this is wicked, put me down for plenty of it. It accompanies absolutely any main course perfectly and stands up to advance preparation, making it an ideal dinner party dish.

Serves 4

8 large potatoes
50 g (2 oz) butter
1 tablespoon chopped fresh chervil
Oil, for shallow frying
120 ml (4 fl oz) double cream
50 g (2 oz) Gruyère, grated
Salt and freshly ground black pepper

Pre-heat the oven to 200°C/400°F/Gas 6.

Scrub and prick the potatoes then place on a baking tray which has been spread with salt. Bake for 1–1½ hours until cooked.

Cut the potatoes in half, scoop out the flesh and mash. Add the butter and chervil and season with salt and pepper to taste. Divide the mixture into 8 and, with floured hands, shape the mixture to resemble fish cakes.

Heat a little oil in a frying pan and fry the potatoes for 2–3 minutes until golden brown. Place on a baking tray. Make an indent in the centre of each potato, pour in a little cream and top with the grated cheese. Cook under a hot grill until golden brown.

Stir-fried Oriental Vegetables

In this recipe I have used only the ingredients that were available in the home of the gastronomic hostage. The stir-fry could therefore be enhanced by the addition of a few extra ingredients, such as a little oyster sauce, water chestnuts, baby corn and mangetout – in fact, anything that takes your fancy really.

Serves 2

3 tablespoons olive oil
25 g (1 oz) fresh ginger, finely chopped
2 garlic cloves, finely chopped
225 g (8 oz) carrots, finely sliced

225 g (8 oz) onions, finely sliced
175 g (6 oz) leeks, finely sliced
1 bunch of spring onions, sliced
2 red peppers, seeded and sliced
Salt and freshly ground black pepper

Heat the oil in a wok or large frying pan and, when hot, add the ginger and garlic. Cook for 1–2 minutes over a high heat then add the sliced vegetables. Cook for 2–3 minutes, stirring constantly, until still crisp. Season with salt and pepper to taste and serve hot.

Peppers stuffed with Braised Rice

Once again, this is a recipe which cries out for the addition of other ingredients. It is a perfect dish to serve as a hot starter, accompaniment to a main course or adapted slightly as a vegetarian dish. It could be argued that peppers were created just to be stuffed!

Serves 4

4 small peppers, either red or green
Oil, for brushing
225 g (8 oz) Rice Pilaff (page 73)

300 ml (10 fl oz) chicken stock
7 g (¼ oz) arrowroot
Salt and freshly ground black pepper

Brush each pepper with a little oil then cook under a hot grill for 1 minute to loosen the skin. Peel off the skin. Cut open each pepper by slicing off the top (stalk end). Reserve the top. Remove all the seeds and discard. Fill the peppers with the rice and replace the tops. Sit the peppers in a roasting tin, add the stock and cover with foil. Bake for 25–30 minutes until tender. When cooked, transfer the peppers to a serving dish, cover and keep warm.

Place the roasting tin over a high flame, moisten the arrowroot with a little cold water and whisk into the boiling liquid. Season with salt and pepper to taste and pour around the stuffed peppers.

Gratin Dauphinois

❦

This recipe is probably one of the most widely used potato dishes in the restaurant world due to its ease of preparation and ability to retain its quality over a fairly long period of time. I still have a liking for this recipe although it is not too kind to my figure!

Serves 4

450 g (1 lb) King Edward potatoes
1 garlic clove, crushed
2 tablespoons snipped fresh chives
150 ml (5 fl oz) double cream
150 ml (5 fl oz) milk

Freshly grated nutmeg
50 g (2 oz) butter, melted
50 g (2 oz) Parmesan, grated
Salt and freshly ground black pepper

Pre-heat the oven to 160°C/325°F/Gas 3.

Peel and thinly slice the potatoes. Wash in cold water then dry on kitchen paper. In a buttered casserole arrange half the potatoes in a layer, sprinkling the garlic, chives, salt and pepper on top. Add the remaining potatoes and season with salt and pepper to taste.

Mix together the cream and milk and season lightly with salt, pepper and nutmeg. Pour the mixture over the potatoes and brush the top with melted butter.

Bake for 1½ hours until the potatoes are tender. Sprinkle the cheese over the surface and cook for a further 10 minutes until golden brown.

French-style Peas

This recipe is ideal for transforming an everyday bag of frozen peas into something quite special. If you are preparing the dish for a vegetarian, simply use a good vegetable stock.

Serves 4

8 button onions, skinned
1 small lettuce, finely shredded
450 g (1 lb) small peas
65 g (2½ oz) butter

Pinch of sugar
600 ml (1 pint) chicken stock
25 g (1 oz) plain flour
Salt

Put the onions, lettuce, peas, 25 g (1 oz) of butter and the sugar in a pan. Add enough stock to just cover then bring to the boil. Cover and simmer gently for about 20 minutes until the onions and peas are tender.

Mix together the remaining 40 g (1½ oz) of the butter and the flour to a smooth paste. Add the paste, in small quantities, to the liquid and gently stir together until the stock thickens. Season with salt to taste before serving.

Spinach cooked with Smoked Bacon in a Light Cream Sauce

❧✿❧

Spinach used to be hard work to prepare. It was often felt that half of the Sahara Desert had to be washed out of it! So these days of ready-washed spinach means that there is no excuse for not using fresh spinach.

Serves 4

900 g (2 lb) spinach, chopped
50 g (2 oz) butter
50 g (2 oz) smoked bacon

300 ml (10 fl oz) double cream
Freshly grated nutmeg
Salt and freshly ground black pepper

Cook the spinach, in just the water that clings to the leaves after washing, for about 5 minutes until tender. Drain and refresh under cold running water. Drain and squeeze to remove all the water.

Heat the butter in a pan, add the bacon and cook until browned. Add the spinach and season with nutmeg, salt and pepper. Pour in the cream, mix well together and heat through before serving.

Almond Potatoes

— ❧ —

It is a good idea to make lots of these on a cold rainy day. Bag and freeze them and then benefit from your efforts for months to come.

Serves 4

450 g (1 lb) large potatoes
25 g (1 oz) butter
2 egg yolks
1 tablespoon snipped fresh chives

2 eggs, beaten
100 g (4 oz) flaked almonds
Oil, for deep frying
Salt and freshly ground black pepper

Peel and cut the potatoes into smallish, even-sized pieces. Put in a pan of cold salted water, bring to the boil and simmer for 15–20 minutes until tender. Drain and return the potatoes to a low heat to dry them. Mash the potatoes well and add the butter, egg yolks and chives. Season with salt and pepper to taste. Leave to cool.

With floured hands, shape the potato in balls the size of an apricot. Dip in the beaten egg then coat in the flaked almonds. Heat the oil in a deep-fat fryer to 190°C/375°F and fry the potatoes for 1 minute until golden brown. Serve hot.

Biarritz Potatoes

If ever there was a potato dish worthy of being eaten as a single dish, it is this one. Lovely flavours, refreshing colour combinations and a variance in textures makes this a firm favourite in our house. Be sure to dry the potatoes as stated in the recipe or you will lose much of the flavour.

Serves 4

450 g (1 lb) King Edward potatoes
75 g (3 oz) butter
2 egg yolks
75 g (3 fl oz) double cream
25 g (1 oz) red pepper, seeded and finely diced

25 g (1 oz) green pepper, seeded and finely diced
50 g (2 oz) cooked ham, finely diced
Salt and white pepper
Freshly grated nutmeg

Peel and cut the potatoes into smallish, even-sized pieces. Put in a pan of cold salted water, bring to the boil and simmer for 15–20 minutes until tender. Drain and return the potatoes to a low heat to dry them.

Mash the potatoes and add the butter and egg yolks. Mix well together then stir in the cream. Add the peppers and cooked ham. Season to taste with the salt, pepper and grated nutmeg. Transfer to a serving dish.

BAKES AND CAKES

As a nation we have been deprived of our home-baking skills because of various social and economic factors, including the introduction of very good in-house bakeries in many of the large supermarkets. It's such a shame because there's something very comforting in the smell of goods baking in the oven at home. The following recipes are interesting and easy to follow and should inspire your whole family to start baking.

I always feel an urge to bake if it's a stormy day. I'm not sure if this is a hang-up from my childhood but I find the process very comforting, a little therapeutic and in our house it has become a bit of a tradition.

It is a sensible idea to have a bulk-bake day. Make and bake lots of different things all at the same time. This is energy-saving and makes excellent use of your time. It really is just as easy to make 4 cakes on the same day as it is to make one. And as most households stock the ingredients required to make biscuits and cakes as standard essential items, such as flour, baking powder, sugar and eggs, there really is no excuse for not baking!

Baked goods generally retain their freshness if stored in an airtight container, some, particularly fruit cakes, improve with age. I only wish I had!

Rich Fruit Cake

Here's a simple recipe for a classic cake – perfect with a cup of tea.

Serves 12

225 g (8 oz) sultanas
450 g (1 lb) currants
100 g (4 oz) raisins
4 tablespoons brandy
225 g (8 oz) plain flour
¼ teaspoon nutmeg
¼ teaspoon cinnamon
¼ teaspoon mixed spice
½ teaspoon salt
225 g (8 oz) unsalted butter
225 g (8 oz) brown sugar

4 eggs, beaten
50 g (2 oz) glacé cherries, finely
    chopped
75 g (3 oz) mixed peel, finely
    chopped
25 g (1 oz) flaked almonds
25 g (1 oz) broken walnuts,
    chopped
Grated rind of 1 lemon
Grated rind of 1 orange

Soak the dried fruit in the brandy for at least 12 hours.

Pre-heat the oven to 140°C/275°F/Gas 1.

Grease and line a 20-cm (8-in) round cake tin and tie a band of corrugated brown paper around the outside. Sift the flour, spices and salt into a large mixing bowl. Put the butter and sugar into another bowl and beat together until light and fluffy. Gradually add the eggs, a little at a time, to prevent the mixture from curdling, and whisk together.

Once the eggs have been incorporated, fold in the flour using a metal spoon. Add the soaked fruit, the cherries, peel, nuts, lemon and orange rind and mix well together. Transfer the mixture to the prepared tin and cover the top of the cake with a double layer of greaseproof paper. Bake for 4–4½ hours until a skewer inserted in the centre comes out clean.

Leave to cool in the tin then remove, wrap in greaseproof paper and store in an airtight container for at least 2 weeks before eating.

Shortbread

Not just for the festive season but all year round. This is the perfect recipe for the children to experiment with as their first step into the kitchen.

Makes 24 fingers

225 g (8 oz) plain flour
100 g (4 oz) cornflour
225 g (8 oz) unsalted butter

100 g (4 oz) caster sugar plus extra
to dust
1 teaspoon rose water

Pre-heat the oven to 150°C/300°F/Gas 2.

Grease a shallow rectangular tin. Sift together the flour and cornflour into a bowl and rub in the butter until the mixture binds together. Add the sugar and the rose water and mix to form a dough.

Transfer to the prepared tin, mark into finger lengths and prick the surface with a fork. Bake for 12–15 minutes until golden brown. Cool on a wire rack. Dust with caster sugar.

Cheese Biscuits

These are just as they sound – cheese biscuits! Ideal to serve with cheese or simply as a snack by themselves.

Makes about 24

50 g (2 oz) plain flour
50 g (2 oz) Parmesan, grated
50 g (2 oz) Cheddar, grated

50 g (2 oz) butter
1 tablespoon milk
Salt and freshly ground black pepper

Pre-heat the oven to 180°C/350°F/Gas 4.

Sift together the flour and ¼ teaspoon salt into a bowl. Then add the pepper. Add the Parmesan and Cheddar and butter. Using the tips of the fingers, rub together to form a dough. If necessary, add the milk to bind the mixture together. On a lightly floured surface, roll out the dough until 3 mm (⅛ in) thick, then, using a 2.5-cm (1-in) plain cutter, cut into rounds. Place on a baking tray and bake for about 15 minutes, until pale golden. Cool on a wire rack.

Jam Sponge

❧❀❧

A trouble-free, classic recipe which every child should be taught at an early age. It's so simple and always works so it's great as a culinary motivator. Store the sponge in an airtight container and it will keep for 3–4 days.

Serves 6

*175 g (6 oz) butter, at room
   temperature*
175 g (6 oz) caster sugar
3 eggs, beaten

Vanilla essence
175 g (6 oz) self-raising flour, sifted
Jam, to fill
Icing sugar, to decorate

Pre-heat the oven to 190°C/375°F/Gas 5.

Grease two 18-cm (7-in) sandwich tins and line the base of each with grease-proof paper. In a large bowl, beat together the butter and sugar until light and fluffy. Add a little egg whilst whisking and, once thoroughly blended, add a little more. Continue to do this until all of the egg has been added. Mix in a few drops of the vanilla essence then, using a metal spoon, gradually fold in the flour, a small amount at a time. If the consistency is correct, the mixture should fall from the spoon. If not, add a little hot water and mix together.

Divide the mixture between the prepared tins and level the surface. Bake for about 20 minutes until risen and golden brown. Turn out and cool on a wire rack. When cold, sandwich the cakes together with jam and sift icing sugar over the top.

Oatcakes

———————— ❧❀❧ ————————

These are so easy to make and, stored in an airtight container, will last, although I always find that they are eaten before there's time to get them into storage!

Makes about 36

225 g (8 oz) plain flour
½ teaspoon salt
½ teaspoon bicarbonate of soda
225 g (8 oz) porridge oats

75 g (3 oz) margarine or butter
75 g (3 oz) lard
75 g (3 oz) caster sugar
A little milk, to moisten

Pre-heat the oven to 200°C/400°F/Gas 6.

Sift the flour, salt and bicarbonate of soda into a bowl. Add the oats and rub in the margarine and lard. Mix in the sugar. Make a well in the centre, add a little milk and draw the mixture together to form a dough.

On a lightly floured surface, roll out the dough until 3 mm (⅛ in) thick. Using a plain 7.5-cm (3-in) round cutter, cut into biscuits.

Place onto a heated baking tray and bake for about 10 minutes until golden brown. Cool on a wire rack, then store in an airtight container.

Tuiles

———————— ❧❀❧ ————————

These little biscuits are usually served with a rich dessert. Make them in advance and store in an airtight container.

Makes 25–30

2 egg whites
100 g (4 oz) caster sugar
50 g (2 oz) plain flour, sifted

50 g (2 oz) butter, melted
A drop of vanilla essence

Pre-heat the oven to 180°C/350°F/Gas 4.

Line a baking tray with baking parchment.

Put the egg whites into a large mixing bowl. Whisk in the sugar, followed by the flour and finally add the butter and vanilla essence. Ensure that all the ingredients are well mixed together.

Place teaspoonfuls of the mixture onto the prepared baking tray, leaving plenty of space between each portion in order to allow for spreading.

Bake for about 6–8 minutes until golden brown. Remove from the tray using a palette knife and place over an orange or upturned teacup to shape the biscuits. When cold, store in an airtight container.

Easy Sponge Cake

This is a throw-it-together recipe and always produces a lovely sponge. It should be eaten as soon as possible after it has been baked.

Serves 6–8

FOR THE SPONGE:
100 g (4 oz) self-raising flour
1 teaspoon baking powder
100 g (4 oz) soft margarine
100 g (4 oz) caster sugar
2 size 1 eggs
A drop of vanilla essence

TO FINISH:
3–4 tablespoons seedless jam
150 ml (5 fl oz) double cream,
* lightly whipped*
Icing sugar, to dust

Pre-heat the oven to 160°C/325°F/Gas 3.

Grease and base-line 2 x 18-cm (7-in) sandwich cake tins. Sift the flour and baking powder into a large mixing bowl. Add the remaining ingredients and, using an electric hand whisk, mix together until well blended.

Turn the mixture into the prepared tins and bake for about 30 minutes until well risen and firm to the touch. Turn out and cool on a wire rack.

When cold, sandwich the cakes together with jam and cream. Dust the top with icing sugar and indulge yourself!

Parkin

——————— ❧❦❧ ———————

This, along with gingerbread, is a brilliant accompaniment to cheese. It is best eaten after having been stored for at least two weeks in an airtight container.

Serves 9

100 g (4 oz) golden syrup
25 g (1 oz) black treacle
75 g (3 oz) block margarine or butter
75 g (3 oz) brown sugar
175 g (6 oz) oatmeal

75 g (3 oz) self-raising flour
2 teaspoons ground ginger
Pinch of salt
1 egg, lightly beaten
1 dessertspoon milk

Pre-heat the oven to 140°C/275°F/Gas 1.

Lightly grease a 15-cm (6-in) square cake tin. Put the syrup, treacle, margarine and sugar in a pan and heat gently until the margarine has melted.

Put the oatmeal, flour, ginger and salt into a bowl and gradually add the syrup mixture, stirring all the time. Add the egg and milk and mix together.

Pour the mixture into the prepared tin and bake for about 1½ hours until firm to the touch. Leave to cool in the tin, then turn out and store in an airtight container.

Plain Scones

❦

This fail-proof recipe will produce lovely, moist scones. They are enhanced when split and filled with jam and cream.

Makes 12

225 g (8 oz) self-raising flour
40 g (1½ oz) butter
40 g (1½ oz) caster sugar

Pinch of salt
150 ml (5 fl oz) milk
1 egg, lightly beaten

Pre-heat the oven to 220°C/425°F/Gas 7.

Grease a large baking tray. Sift the flour into a bowl, add the butter and rub in until the mixture resembles breadcrumbs. Stir in the sugar and salt and add the milk, a little at a time, to form a soft dough. If necessary, add a little more milk if the mixture feels dry.

On a lightly floured surface, knead the dough lightly to remove any cracks, then roll it out until 2 cm (¾ in) thick. Using a 5-cm (2-in) plain round cutter, cut out the dough into scones. Gather up the trimmings into a dough, roll out and cut into scones.

Place on the prepared baking tray and brush the tops of the scones with the beaten egg. Bake for 10–14 minutes until golden brown and firm to the touch. Cool on a wire rack.

Parmesan and Paprika Scones

❦

Great on a cold winter's day in with a crackling fire and a good video.

Makes 8

75 g (3 oz) self-raising flour, sifted
75 g (3 oz) wholemeal flour
25 g (1 oz) butter
1 size 2 egg, beaten
3 tablespoons cold milk

100 g (4 oz) Parmesan, freshly
* grated*
1 teaspoon paprika
1 tablespoon finely chopped fresh
* parsley*
Salt and freshly ground black pepper

Pre-heat the oven to 220°C/425°F/Gas 7.

Mix the two flours together and rub in the butter until the mixture resembles breadcrumbs. Make a well in the centre and add the egg and milk. Stir together and draw the sides into the liquid and mix. Add the cheese, paprika, parsley, a pinch of salt and pepper and mix to a smooth dough.

Place the dough onto a lightly floured surface and roll out to a thickness of 2 cm (¾ in) then, using a 5.5-cm (2¼-in) round cutter, cut into scones.

Place onto a floured baking sheet and cook in the oven for 15–20 minutes until risen and golden brown.

Original Gingerbread

❧✻❧

I like to serve this with Stilton and a handful of chilled grapes.

Makes 9–12

---

225 g (8 oz) plain flour
1 teaspoon baking powder
1 teaspoon ground ginger
100 g (4 oz) butter, cut into cubes
100 g (4 oz) demerara sugar

1 tablespoon golden syrup, warmed
25 g (1 oz) sultanas
25 g (1 oz) stem ginger, finely
  chopped
40 g (1½ oz) granulated sugar

Pre-heat the oven to 150°C/300°F/Gas 2.

Lightly grease and line a 20-cm (8-in) square cake tin.

Sift the flour, baking powder and ground ginger into a bowl. Add the butter and rub in until the mixture resembles breadcrumbs. Mix in the demerara sugar, add the syrup and mix together. Finally, mix in the sultanas and ginger.

Turn the mixture into the prepared tin and lightly cover the surface with the granulated sugar. Bake for 40–45 minutes until firm to the touch.

Leave to cool in the tin, then turn out and cut into small squares.

HOT PUDDINGS

Hot puddings for me conjure up memories of my school days – rainy, stressful (I wasn't the best behaved pupil!) but with highlighted moments around 12.30 p.m. each day. This was the point at which bread and butter pudding, spotted dick, steamed jam pudding, tapioca and a host of other delights graced the school's dining tables.

It always seemed that the main meal was inedible but the puddings were wonderful and the effect it had on me was to leave me lusting after the talents of the pastry cook! I hope you enjoy the recipes in this chapter as much as I do!

Zabaglione alla Marsala

This classical Italian dessert is one of the easiest puddings ever created. I find that a small glass of dessert wine makes it much more digestible and even more enjoyable. Served with a bowl of fresh strawberries, it is difficult to beat.

Serves 4

4 egg yolks
150 g (5 oz) caster sugar
4 tablespoons Marsala

Thinly sliced rind and juice of ½ a lemon
4 mint leaves, to decorate
Shortbread or sponge finger, to serve

Put the egg yolks and sugar in a large heatproof bowl and whisk well together. Add the Marsala and lemon juice. Place the bowl over a pan of simmering water and whisk until the mixture is pale and has at least doubled in volume and clings to the whisk when the whisk is raised.

Pour the zabaglione into glasses and decorate with lemon rind and mint leaves. Serve immediately with shortbread or sponge fingers.

Warm Lemon Tart

———— ❧❖❧ ————

This is without a shadow of a doubt one of the most delightful puddings you could wish to eat. It can be further enhanced by serving with fresh Custard Sauce (page 169) to which a little almond essence has been added or, better still, some marzipan broken up and whisked into the hot custard. Flood the plate with the sauce, add the tart and, if wished, serve with Walnut Ice-cream (page 175).

Serves 4–6

FOR THE PASTRY:
175 g (6 oz) plain flour
25 g (1 oz) icing sugar
75 g (3 oz) unsalted butter
1 egg yolk
1 tablespoon cold water

FOR THE FILLING:
4 lemons
3 eggs
75 g (3 oz) caster sugar
75 ml (3 fl oz) double cream
A little icing sugar, to dust

To make the pastry, sift the flour and sugar in a bowl. Add the butter and rub in until the mixture resembles breadcrumbs. Make a hollow in the centre and add the egg and water. Mix together to form a smooth ball. Wrap in foil and put in the fridge to rest for at least 1 hour.

Pre-heat the oven to 200°C/400°F/Gas 6.

On a lightly floured surface, roll out the pastry and use to line a 2.5-cm (1-in) deep 20-cm (8-in) flan dish. Using a fork, prick the base of the flan to prevent it from rising during baking and line with foil. Bake for 10–15 minutes until set.

Meanwhile, prepare the filling. Grate the lemons and squeeze out the juice. (You will need no more than 175 ml (6 fl oz) of juice, so feel free to drink any surplus!) Lightly whisk the eggs and sugar together, add the lemon juice and grated rind, reserving a little for decorating, and finally the cream. Continue mixing until well blended, but do be careful not to overmix.

Remove the pastry case from the oven and reduce the temperature to 180°C/350°F/Gas 4. Pour the filling into the pastry case and return to the oven. Cook for a further 25–30 minutes until the mixture has set and feels firm to the touch. Dust with icing sugar and decorate with the reserved lemon rind.

Queen of Puddings

❧❀❧

I opted for this dish following the abduction of a shopper in Kent who had purchased eggs and sugar. She was quite adamant that she could not make puddings and that even though her family thoroughly enjoyed them, it wasn't worth the effort because they never turned out as nice as they sounded. This recipe converted her. It's so simple to make, relatively inexpensive and comforting to eat, just as all good puddings should be. It cries out for a jug of custard and half an hour's sleep after eating it!

Serves 4

450 ml (15 fl oz) milk
1 vanilla pod
150 ml (5 fl oz) double cream
100 g (4 oz) fresh white bread
   crumbs

25 g (1 oz) unsalted butter
75 g (3 oz) caster sugar
Grated rind of ½ a lemon
2 size 1 eggs
4 tablespoons raspberry jam

Put the milk, vanilla pod and cream in a pan and bring to the boil. Remove from the heat and mix in the breadcrumbs and butter. Add 25 g (1 oz) of the sugar and the lemon rind. Mix together, cover and leave for 1 hour until cold.

Pre-heat the oven to 180°C/350°F/Gas 4.

Butter a 900-ml (1½-pint) ovenproof dish. Separate the eggs. When the milk and breadcrumb mixture is cold, mix in the egg yolks and transfer to the prepared dish. Bake for 25–30 minutes until set. Warm the jam in a pan until melted then sieve over the surface of the pudding. Whisk the egg whites until stiff, quickly whisk in 25 g (1 oz) of sugar, then pour over the pudding.

Coat the surface of the meringue with the remaining 25 g (1 oz) of sugar. Bake for a further 10–12 minutes until golden brown.

Bread and Butter Pudding with Whisky Cream

—————————— ❦ ——————————

No collection of pudding recipes is complete without this little number.
The use of double cream is very extravagant, both on the hips and the pocket,
but I think for this it's well worth suffering.

Serves 4

150 ml (5 fl oz) double cream
1 vanilla pod
2 eggs
50 g (2 oz) caster sugar
8 large slices white bread
50 g (2 oz) butter
25 g (1 oz) currants
25 g (1 oz) sultanas

Grated rind of ½ a small lemon
Grated rind of ½ a small orange

FOR THE WHISKY CREAM:
125 ml (4 fl oz) double cream
1 tablespoon whisky
1 tablespoon clear honey

Put 150 ml (5 fl oz) of the cream and the vanilla pod into a pan and heat without boiling. Whisk together the eggs and sugar, add the cream, mix well and strain into a jug.

Using a plain round cutter, cut the bread into 8 rounds: 4 to fit individual ramekin dishes and 4 to fit on top. Butter 4 rounds of the bread on one side and the other 4 on both sides. Use the remaining butter to grease the ramekin dishes. Line with the bread buttered on both sides then half-fill with the egg and cream mixture. Add the currants, sultanas, lemon and orange rind. Place a round of bread on top, buttered side uppermost, cover and leave for 15 minutes.

Pre-heat the oven to 180°C/350°F/Gas 4.

Fill the dishes with the remaining egg and cream mixture. Stand the dishes in a roasting tin filled with enough hot water to come halfway up the sides of the dishes. Bake for 20–25 minutes until firm to the touch but not brown.

Meanwhile, make the whisky cream. Lightly whisk together the 125 ml (4 fl oz) of cream, the whisky and honey. Put the whisky cream into individual ramekin dishes and serve a dish, with a pudding alongside, on a large plate.

Poached Stuffed Pears glazed with a Sabayon Sauce

❧❀❧

Be sure to select perfectly formed pears for this dish and peel them carefully in order to retain their shape. The concept of stuffing pears gives a lovely dimension to the dish, an element of surprise! The good thing about using the Sabayon sauce is that you are free to choose whether to glaze the finished dish under the grill or leave it plain. It looks just as lovely either way.

Serves 4

4 Comice pears
75 g (3 oz) granulated sugar
1 vanilla pod
1 ripe peach
1 x 20-cm (8-in) sponge cake
3 egg yolks

100 g (4 oz) caster sugar
Grated rind and juice of ½ a
    lemon
4 tablespoons sherry
25 g (1 oz) flaked almonds
4 mint leaves, to decorate

Peel the pears, retaining the stalk. Put the sugar, vanilla pod and 300 ml (10 fl oz) water in a pan, bring to the boil then reduce the heat to enable the liquid to simmer. Add the pears, cover with a lid and cook gently for about 15 minutes until just tender. Carefully remove from the liquid, cover and leave to cool slightly. Peel and stone the peach, then very finely dice the flesh. Using an apple corer or a teaspoon, very carefully remove the core from the base of the pears, forming a space inside the fruit into which to pack the diced peach. Fill the pears with the chopped peach.

Using a round cutter, cut out 4 x 5-cm (2-in) rounds from the sponge and place on 4 serving plates. Put the egg yolks into a bowl, add the caster sugar, lemon rind and juice, and sherry. Sit the bowl over a pan of simmering water and whisk until the mixture becomes pale and has doubled in volume. Remove from the heat.

Sit the stuffed pears on top of the sponge and coat each pear with the Sabayon sauce. If wished, cook under a hot grill until brown then serve decorated with the flaked almonds and mint leaves.

Crêpes Normande

I'm not normally a pancake fan, but this one's lovely. Do try to keep the batter
as light as possible when adding it to the pan; the tendency is to wait
to pour it in. If you do, you could end up with a dish more likely
to cover the wheels of Nigel Mansell's racing car!

Serves 4

275 g (10 oz) plain flour
Pinch of salt
40 g (1½ oz) caster sugar plus a
   little, to serve
2 size 6 eggs

300 ml (10 fl oz) milk
50 g (2 oz) butter
350 g (12 oz) Granny Smith apples
1 teaspoon cinnamon
4 tablespoons calvados

Sift together the flour and salt in a bowl. Add 15 g (½ oz) of the sugar and eggs
then the milk. Whisk until smooth. Melt 25 g (1 oz) of the butter and whisk
into the batter. Chill for at least 1 hour.

Peel, core and dice the apples. Heat the remaining 25 g (1 oz) butter in a deep
pan and add the apples, cinnamon, calvados and the remaining 25 g (1 oz) of
sugar. Cook for 5 minutes until soft then remove from the heat.

Heat a lightly oiled pancake pan and add about one-eighth of the batter, just
enough to coat the base of the pan, and cook for 2–3 seconds until just beginning to set. Spread a quarter of the apple mixture over the surface of the batter
and then cover with the same amount of batter as originally used.

Once the base has cooked and is brown then very carefully turn the crêpe
over (no tossing!) and cook the other side. Once cooked, transfer onto a plate
and dust with sugar before serving. Repeat with the remaining batter and apple
mixture to make 4 crêpes.

Cherry Clafoutis

This is not unlike a sweet version of Yorkshire pudding and you can use any fruit in season. It does need to be eaten fresh from the oven and benefits from being served with a spoonful of clotted cream.

Serves 4–6

225 g (8 oz) plain flour
Pinch of salt
½ teaspoon baking powder
3 eggs, lightly beaten
50 g (2 oz) caster sugar plus a little,
    to serve

150 ml (5 fl oz) milk
40 g (1½ oz) unsalted butter,
    melted
450 g (1 lb) ripe dark cherries,
    stoned

Pre-heat the oven to 180°C/350°F/Gas 4.

Butter a 25-cm (10-in) flan dish. Sift the flour, salt and baking powder into a bowl, make a hollow in the centre and add the eggs, sugar, milk and butter. Mix well to form a smooth batter. Pour into the prepared dish and scatter the cherries on top.

Cook for 50 minutes–1 hour until set and lightly browned. Sprinkle lightly with sugar and serve warm.

Rhubarb and Ginger Crumble with a Bay Leaf Custard

❧❀❧

This would be one of the things I would take on a desert island. It's a pudding that draws on all that is good about British cookery. The bay leaf custard is delightful as an accompaniment to the rhubarb flavour.

Serves 4

675 g (1½ lb) rhubarb
100 g (4 oz) brown sugar
A piece of stem ginger, preserved in
   syrup, grated
100 g (4 oz) plain flour
¼ teaspoon baking powder
40 g (1½ oz) unsalted butter

FOR THE CUSTARD:
300 ml (10 fl oz) milk
2 large bay leaves
3 eggs, lightly beaten
100 g (4 oz) caster sugar

Chop the rhubarb into 2.5-cm (1-in) pieces, place into a deep pan and add 50 g (2 oz) of the sugar and ginger. Cook gently for 10–12 minutes until tender, stirring occasionally. Put into a baking dish.

Pre-heat the oven to 180°C/350°F/Gas 4.

Sift together the flour and baking powder. Stir in the remaining 50 g (2 oz) of sugar then rub in the butter until the mixture resembles breadcrumbs. Put the crumble mixture on top of the fruit. Bake for 35–40 minutes until golden brown.

To make the custard, bring the milk to the boil. Add the bay leaves and pour onto the eggs in a bowl. Beat well together then add the sugar. Sit the bowl over a pan of simmering water and stir continuously until the sauce thickens. Remove the bay leaves and serve with the crumble.

Ragout of Peaches spiced with Cinnamon

❧❀❧

This dish was created out of a chance meeting in a large supermarket between myself and an elderly gentleman who had acquired a basket of peaches and nothing else. The cinnamon really develops the full flavour of the fruit and the Walnut Ice-cream is an essential element to the dish, even if you have to buy it.

Serves 4

50 g (2 oz) butter
4 fresh peaches, skinned, halved and
  stoned
75 g (3 oz) soft brown sugar
Pinch of cinnamon

Finely grated rind and juice of
  1 orange
Finely grated rind of ½ a lemon
4 tablespoons brandy
Walnut Ice-cream (page 175), to serve
4 sprigs of mint, to decorate

Heat the butter in a frying pan, add the peaches and cook for 2 minutes on both sides. Add the sugar and cinnamon and continue to cook until the sugar has dissolved, but before it turns to caramel.

Add the orange and lemon rind, pour in the brandy and carefully set alight to burn off the alcohol, then add the orange juice. When the liquid begins to boil, reduce the heat and simmer for 1–2 minutes until syrupy in consistency. Serve with ice-cream, decorated with mint leaves.

Chocolate Soufflé with a Strawberry Mint Base

Having been diagnosed by a very senior clinical chocologist as someone with a huge problem in this area, I am most conscious of the need to present chocolate in as many ways as possible. This clever little dish goes some way to disguise the ingredient without losing the taste and it's a foolproof soufflé.

Serves 4

100 g (4 oz) dark chocolate
4 egg yolks, beaten
6 egg whites
75 g (3 oz) strawberries, quartered

1 tablespoon chopped fresh mint
4 tablespoons Amaretto
A little icing sugar, to dust

Pre-heat the oven to 200°C/400°F/Gas 6.

Grease a 1.2-litre (2-pint) soufflé dish generously with butter. Break the chocolate into a heatproof bowl and place over a pan of simmering water. Heat, stirring, until melted and smooth. Remove from the heat and gradually beat in the egg yolks.

Whisk the egg whites until stiff then fold into the chocolate mixture, making sure that they are thoroughly mixed without removing the air from the egg whites.

Put the strawberries, mint and Amaretto in a pan and quickly bring to the boil. Put the strawberry mixture into the prepared dish then add the soufflé mixture. Bake in the oven for 18–20 minutes until well risen and firm to the touch.

Dust the top with icing sugar and serve immediately.

Apple and Mango Charlotte

❧❀❧

The combination of apples and mango is a most interesting one. When I serve this dish I prefer not to tell my guests what they are eating. Keep them guessing!

Serves 4

225 g (8 oz) Bramley apples, peeled, cored and chopped
225 g (8 oz) mango, peeled, stoned and chopped

50 g (2 oz) caster sugar
125 g (5 oz) butter
6 slices of white bread
1 egg yolk

Put the apples, mango, sugar and 25 g (1 oz) of the butter in a pan and cook over a low heat for 15–20 minutes, stirring occasionally, until the fruit is tender. Using a wooden spoon, beat well together then set aside.

Melt the remaining 100 g (4 oz) of butter. Remove the crusts from each slice of bread then brush with the melted butter on both sides. Using 4½ slices of the bread, line a 600-ml (1-pint) pudding basin, making sure to slightly overlap each slice, leaving no gaps.

Beat the egg yolk into the apple and mango mixture and use to fill the pudding basin. Seal the top with the remaining 1½ slices of bread, again ensuring there are no gaps. Place an appropriate-sized ovenproof plate on top of the pudding and sit a heavy weight on the plate. Leave to stand for 1 hour.

Pre-heat the oven to 200°C/400°F/Gas 6.

Bake the pudding with the weight still on top for 30–35 minutes. Remove the weight and plate and return the pudding to the oven for a further 10 minutes until the top is browned. Leave to stand for a few minutes then carefully turn out onto a plate and serve.

Treacle Tart with Clotted Cream

Without a doubt, this is one of the most classic of English dishes that I could choose. It is a pudding which demands two things of you, firstly to devour an extra portion and secondly to work hard at losing those extra calories. It's just as good hot or cold.

Serves 4–6

FOR THE PASTRY:
350 g (12 oz) plain flour
Pinch of salt
125 g (5 oz) butter, chilled
1 egg, beaten

FOR THE FILLING:
1 apple
50 g (2 oz) fresh breadcrumbs
4 tablespoons golden syrup
Grated rind and juice of 1 lemon
1 egg, lightly beaten
4 tablespoons double cream
Beaten egg, to glaze
Clotted cream, to serve

To make the pastry, sift the flour and salt into a large bowl. Add the butter and rub in until the mixture resembles breadcrumbs. Make a hollow in the centre, add the beaten egg and 3–4 tablespoons chilled water and mix together to form a firm, smooth dough but do not over-handle. Place the pastry in a plastic bag and chill for at least 2 hours.

Pre-heat the oven to 190°C/375°F/Gas 5.

Allow the pastry to reach room temperature then roll out on a lightly floured surface and use to line a 20-cm (8-in) flan ring. Put the pastry trimmings in the fridge for use later in the recipe. Using a fork, prick the base of the flan and line with foil. Bake for about 10 minutes until set.

To make the filling, peel, core and grate the apple then add to the breadcrumbs. Warm the syrup, then add to the breadcrumb mixture with the lemon rind and juice, beaten egg and cream. Mix well together, then pour into the pastry case. Make strips from the reserved pastry and place these over the tart in a lattice pattern. Brush the pastry with the beaten egg and bake for a further 20–25 minutes until just set and golden brown. Serve with as much clotted cream as you dare!

COLD PUDDINGS

If I didn't have a wife to control my weight I would probably eat myself to death, especially on cold and hot puddings and those with double cream or chocolate.

If puddings are important in your household and time is limited, it's a good idea to find a recipe which has a standard base, such as Walnut Ice-cream (opposite) or the Lemon and Pistachio Soufflé (see page 182) in this book, and double the quantities. Make half into a pudding for that day but add extra ingredients to the remainder of the mixture in order to have a different pudding for the following day. An example would be to add chopped walnuts and a glass of sherry to the lemon soufflé. Easy but effective.

Lemon Cheesecake

It is hard to imagine anything more traditional than a lemon cheesecake and isn't it lovely that in an ever-changing world some things do remain the same. This dish was made by an eight-year-old girl called Amanda, assisted by me.

Serves 6

100 g (4 oz) digestive biscuits
50 g (2 oz) butter
350 g (12 oz) cottage cheese
65 g (2½ oz) caster sugar
2 egg yolks

Grated rind and juice of 2 lemons
15 g (½ oz) powdered gelatine
3 tablespoons water
150 ml (5 fl oz) double cream
Grapes and mint leaves, to decorate

Finely crush the biscuits. Melt the butter, add the biscuits and mix well together. Press the mixture into a 20-cm (8-in) loose-bottomed cake tin. Place in the fridge. Blend the cottage cheese and sugar together in a food processor until smooth. Add the egg yolks and lemon rind and juice. Sprinkle the gelatine over the water in a small bowl and leave to soak for 5 minutes. Place the bowl over a pan of simmering water and stir until dissolved. Add to the cheese mixture and blend well together. Whip the cream until it just holds its shape then fold into the cheese mixture.

Pour the mixture onto the biscuit base then chill in the fridge for about 3 hours until set. To serve, carefully remove from the tin and garnish with grapes and mint leaves.

Walnut Ice-cream

There's no doubt that freshly made ice-cream is nicer than the commercially produced product and it is, in my opinion, well worth investing in a domestic ice-cream-making machine. However, this recipe works on the assumption that most people don't own one and demonstrates that it is still feasible to make your own and compete with the 'big names'. Incidentally, it's a wonderful accompaniment to the Warm Lemon Tart on page 163.

Serves 6

3 egg yolks
75 g (3 oz) Muscovado sugar
50 g (2 oz) broken walnuts, chopped

300 ml (10 fl oz) milk
300 ml (10 fl oz) double cream

In a heatproof bowl, whisk together the egg yolks and sugar until pale in colour and thick in texture. Add the chopped walnuts. Bring the milk to the boil then whisk into the egg yolk mixture. Stand the bowl over a pan of simmering water for 12–15 minutes, stirring, until it thickens. Remove from the heat and strain into a bowl. Cover with a piece of greaseproof paper to prevent a skin from forming and leave until cold.

Add the double cream and mix well. Place the bowl in a freezer and leave for about 3 hours. Remove and whisk the ice-cream to ensure that the ice crystals around the edge are distributed evenly. Return to the freezer for a further 2 hours and repeat the process.

Transfer the ice-cream to a freezer container and freeze for 2–3 hours until firm. Transfer the ice-cream to a fridge 30 minutes before being served, to soften it slightly.

White and Dark Chocolate Marquise with Coffee Cream

A real chocaholic's delight. The result is pleasing to the eye but heavy on the waistline. However, well worth it in my view.

Serves 8

FOR THE MARQUISE:
1 packet of Langue de Chat biscuits
4 tablespoons rum
225 g (8 oz) dark chocolate
275 g (10 oz) white chocolate
550 ml (18 fl oz) double cream

FOR THE COFFEE CREAM:
2 teaspoons instant coffee
1 teaspoon boiling water
300 ml (10 fl oz) double cream
1 teaspoon caster sugar

TO DECORATE:
Mint leaves
Icing sugar

Line a 450-g (1-lb) loaf tin with greaseproof paper and brush with oil. Briefly dip the biscuits in the rum and use to line the bottom and sides of the tin, facing the rounded pale side inwards. Reserve some biscuits for the top.

Break the chocolate into 2 separate heatproof bowls and place each over a pan of simmering water. Heat until melted then remove from the heat. Stir 300 ml (10 fl oz) of the cream into the dark chocolate and 250 ml (8 fl oz) of the cream into the white chocolate. Pour half the dark chocolate and half the white chocolate mixtures into the tin, then repeat these layers. Leave in the fridge to set for at least 1½ hours.

To make the coffee cream, stir the coffee into the boiling water until dissolved then mix together with the cream and sugar.

To serve, turn out the marquise and cut into thick slices. Flood serving plates with the coffee cream, place a slice of marquise on top and decorate with mint leaves and a dusting of sifted icing sugar.

Mont Blanc

❧❀❧

A dessert which must be eaten with a glass of chilled dry white wine or, better still, champagne. Chestnuts have a distinct flavour but the dish can leave you feeling thirsty, so indulge yourself from the beginning. In fact, it's probably sensible to have a glass whilst preparing the dish!

Serves 4

450 g (1 lb) chestnuts
500 ml (17 fl oz) milk
100 g (4 oz) granulated sugar
2 egg yolks
1 tablespoon water

50 g (2 oz) unsalted butter
300 ml (10 fl oz) double cream
50 g (2 oz) caster sugar
A few drops of vanilla essence
4 marrons glacés

Pre-heat the oven to 230°C/450°F/Gas 8.

Cut horizontal slits in the shells of the chestnuts. Place them onto a baking tray and bake for 10 minutes until the shells open. Carefully remove the shells and inner skins.

Put the milk and 50 g (2 oz) of the granulated sugar in a pan, add the chestnuts and simmer gently for 20 minutes until they are tender. Drain then blend in a food processor until smooth. Leave to cool.

Put the egg yolks, 50 g (2 oz) of the granulated sugar and the water in a heatproof bowl. Place the bowl over a pan of simmering water and whisk until the mixture is light and fluffy and has doubled in volume. Remove from the heat and beat until the mixture is cold.

Beat the butter until softened then gradually add the egg mixture, a little at a time. Mix the creamed butter mixture into the chestnut purée. Transfer the mixture to a piping bag fitted with a large plain nozzle and pipe into a savarin mould or individual ramekins. Chill until set.

Whip the cream with the 50 g (2 oz) caster sugar and the vanilla essence until it holds its shape. Turn out the Mont Blanc, cover with the cream and decorate with the marrons glacés.

Creamed Nectarines in a Brandy Snap Case

❧❦❧

Of all the programmes from the series, this had to be the biggest production.
Two adults, six children and I created this lovely little pudding.
Now, did they all wash their hands? I hope so!

Serves 8

FOR THE FILLING:
10 nectarines
175 g (6 oz) caster sugar
175 ml (6 fl oz) double cream
1 teaspoon brandy (optional)

FOR THE CASES:
90 g (3½ oz) butter
75 g (3 oz) sugar
120 ml (4 fl oz) golden syrup
1 teaspoon lemon juice
75 g (3 oz) plain flour
½ teaspoon ground ginger

TO DECORATE:
Mint leaves
8 strawberries

To make the filling, immerse the nectarines into a pan of boiling water for
20 seconds then remove and put in a pan of cold water. Peel off the skins then
roughly chop the flesh, discarding the pips. Put into a bowl and add 75 g (3 oz)
of the caster sugar. Cover and leave in the fridge for at least 1 hour.

Drain off the liquid, purée the nectarines in a food processor and sweeten to
taste with the remaining sugar. Whip the cream until it holds its shape then fold
in the nectarine purée. Add the brandy if using. Transfer the purée to the fridge
until required.

To make the brandy snap cases, gently heat the butter, sugar and syrup in a
pan until the sugar has dissolved and then add the lemon juice. Sift together the
flour and ginger then beat into the syrup mixture until smooth. Leave until
cool.

Pre-heat the oven to 200°C/400°F/Gas 6.

Lightly grease a baking tray. Using a teaspoon, place 8 small spoonfuls of the
mixture onto the tray, leaving plenty of room between each spoonful for the
mixture to spread during baking (to about the size of a saucer).

Bake the biscuits for about 5 minutes until golden brown. Remove from the oven and leave to cool for 2 minutes. Using a palette knife, ease the biscuits from the tray and place onto an orange or upturned bowl to shape the cases. Once the shape has been formed then place the biscuits in a dry area until required.

To serve, fill the cases with the purée and decorate with a mint leaf and a strawberry, sliced to form a fan.

Summer Pudding with Kirsch Clotted Cream

⟨❧⟩

This is the epitome of summer. The recipe produces one large pudding but, if you prefer, you could make individual ones. Use small plastic containers as you will find it much easier to turn them out.

Serves 6

225 g (8 oz) redcurrants
75 g (3 oz) blackcurrants
100 g (4 oz) strawberries
450 g (1 lb) raspberries
100 g (4 oz) caster sugar
2 tablespoons kirsch

8 slices of white bread
300 ml (10 fl oz) clotted cream

To DECORATE:
Mint leaves
12 redcurrants

Remove the stalks from the redcurrants and blackcurrants. Hull and quarter the strawberries. Put all the fruit, sugar and 1 tablespoon of the kirsch in a pan and cook over a low heat until the sugar has dissolved. Remove from the heat.

Remove the crusts from the bread and use the bread to line a 900-ml (1½-pint) pudding basin, or 6 individual ramekin dishes, dariole moulds or small plastic containers, ensuring that you leave no space between each piece. Fill with the fruit mixture, reserving a little of the juice for use later. Cover with more bread then sit a plate, or other such item, on top of the pudding itself (not the dish). Place a heavy object on top and chill for at least 8 hours or overnight.

To serve, turn out the pudding and, using a little of the reserved juice, cover any area that looks dry or white. Add the remaining 1 tablespoon of kirsch to the clotted cream and serve a large spoonful with the pudding. Decorate with mint leaves and redcurrants.

Rum Babas

❦

Rich, heavy and wholesome was the description given to this pudding by my victim. It is fair to say that there is a lot of work to do to get them to the table but, as the saying goes, there's no gain without pain.

Makes 6

10 g (¼ oz) fresh yeast
25 ml (1 fl oz) warm milk
225 g (8 oz) plain flour
2 eggs
Pinch of salt
Pinch of sugar
25 g (1 oz) currants
Grated rind of ½ a lemon
25 g (1 oz) sultanas
300 ml (10 fl oz) water
225 g (8 oz) caster sugar

25 g (1 oz) butter
½ an orange, sliced
½ a lemon, sliced
¼ of a cinnamon stick
50 ml (2 fl oz) strong tea
2 tablespoons rum
175 ml (6 fl oz) apricot jam
300 ml (10 fl oz) double cream,
    lightly whipped
8 glacé cherries

Grease 6 dariole moulds. Blend the yeast with the warm milk. Put the flour in a bowl and make a hollow in the centre. Add the eggs, salt and sugar and mix together, blending in a little of the flour. Pour in the yeast liquid and blend in the remaining flour to form a smooth dough. Add the currants, lemon rind and sultanas and mix together. Fill the prepared dariole moulds with the dough until a third full and brush over with the melted butter. Cover with a clean damp cloth and leave to rise in a warm place until the dough reaches the top of the moulds.

Pre-heat the oven to 230°C/450°F/Gas 8.

Bake the rum babas for about 15 minutes until well risen and golden. Cool for a few minutes then turn out onto a wire rack.

Meanwhile, bring the water, 225 g (8 oz) of sugar, sliced fruit, cinnamon, tea and rum to the boil and simmer for 10 minutes. Immerse the babas in the syrup until they become wet without losing their firmness.

Add 3 tablespoons of water to the jam, bring to the boil then sieve into a clean jug. Using a brush, coat the babas with the hot apricot syrup. To serve, split the babas down the centre and fill with whipped cream. Decorate with glacé cherries.

Oeufs à la Neige

❦

There's something very comforting about this dish. Perhaps it's that it provokes memories of a happy childhood, warm custard and fluffy white snow!

Serves 4

4 eggs
Pinch of salt
275 g (10 oz) caster sugar

1 litre (1¾ pints) milk
1 vanilla pod
25 g (1 oz) flaked almonds, toasted

Separate the eggs. Whisk the egg whites with a pinch of salt until stiff. Add 100 g (4 oz) of the sugar and whisk until mixed, then fold in another 100 g (4 oz) of sugar. Bring the milk to the boil with the vanilla pod then reduce the heat and allow the milk to just simmer.

Using 2 tablespoons, spoon on the meringue into 8 even egg shapes. Poach for about 5 minutes until set, turning once. Using a slotted spoon, carefully remove the meringues from the milk, transfer to a plate, cover and keep warm. Reserve the milk but discard the vanilla pod.

Put the egg yolks and the remaining sugar in a heatproof bowl and whisk together until pale and thick. Strain the milk onto the egg mixture and continue whisking until well mixed. Stand the bowl over a pan of simmering water and cook, stirring continuously, until the sauce thickens and coats the back of a wooden spoon. Remove from the heat.

Strain the sauce into a large serving bowl and leave to cool. When cold, place the meringues on the top, sprinkle over the toasted almonds and serve.

Lemon and Pistachio Soufflé

— ❧❀❧ —

Light and fluffy and a sheer delight to eat is the only way to describe this, one of my favourite desserts. It is perfect for dinner parties because it looks as good as it tastes.

Serves 4

10 g (¼ oz) powdered gelatine
Juice of 1½ lemons
2 eggs
100 g (4 oz) caster sugar

75 g (3 oz) pistachio nuts, blanched
  and skinned
175 ml (6 fl oz) double cream
100 g (4 oz) flaked almonds, toasted

Prepare a 1.2-litre (2-pint) soufflé dish with a greaseproof paper collar so that it rises 7.5 cm (3 in) above the top of the dish.

Sprinkle the gelatine over half the lemon juice in a small bowl and leave to soak for 5 minutes. Place the bowl over a pan of simmering water and stir until dissolved. Separate the eggs. Whisk the egg yolks, sugar and remaining lemon juice together in a bowl, over a pan of simmering water until the whisk marks are clearly visible.

Add the dissolved gelatine and allow to cool. Chop the pistachio nuts, reserving 6 to decorate. Mix the chopped nuts into the soufflé mixture. Whip the cream until stiff then fold into the mixture, reserving 3 tablespoons. Whisk the egg whites until stiff and fold into the mixture. Pour into the soufflé dish, allowing the mixture to rise above the top of the dish, retained by the greaseproof paper. (The idea is for the dish to resemble a hot soufflé!) Chill for 4 hours until set.

Remove the paper and coat the edge of the soufflé with the almonds. Pipe a rosette of reserved cream on the centre of the soufflé and decorate with the reserved whole pistachio nuts.

Chilled Chocolate Mousse with Peppered Raspberries

❧❀❧

This began life simply as a bar of chocolate in a shopper's trolley.
Now when it comes to chocolate I'm completely won over. The moment
you add raspberries to it you're onto a winner. Don't be alarmed by
the use of black pepper with the fruit – it really does complement it.

Serves 4

225 g (8 oz) dark chocolate
4 eggs
3 tablespoons brandy
75 g (3 oz) fresh raspberries
Freshly ground black pepper

TO DECORATE:
4 tablespoons double cream, lightly
  whipped
50 g (2 oz) dark chocolate, coarsely
  grated
4 large raspberries
4 small mint leaves

Break the chocolate into a heatproof bowl, stand over a pan of simmering water
and heat until melted. Remove from the heat. Separate the eggs. Lightly beat the
egg yolks then add them to the chocolate. Mix well together then add the
brandy. Leave to cool.

Whisk the egg whites until stiff then, using a metal spoon, very carefully fold
into the chocolate mixture. Sprinkle the raspberries with a very light dusting of
black pepper.

Spoon the mousse mixture into 4 small ramekin dishes to half fill. Put a layer
of the peppered raspberries over the top and then add the remaining mousse
mixture. Chill for 3 hours.

To serve, pipe a rosette of cream on the centre of each mousse, surround with
the grated chocolate and decorate with a raspberry and mint leaf. Indulge yourself!

Banoffi Pie

The credit for this pudding must go to The Hungry Monk restaurant in Jevington, Sussex. The key to the recipe is to ensure that the can of condensed milk is fully immersed in water and that, during the three hours it is being boiled, the water is topped up.

Serves 8

400-g (14-oz) can condensed milk
175 g (6 oz) shortcrust pastry
300 ml (10 fl oz) double cream

1 teaspoon powdered instant coffee
25 g (1 oz) caster sugar
1 large banana

Place the unopened can of condensed milk into a pan of boiling water. Cover and boil for 3 hours, topping up regularly with boiling water. Remove from the water and leave to cool completely before opening.

Pre-heat the oven to 190°C/375°F/Gas 5.

Roll out the pastry on a lightly floured surface and use to line a 20-cm (8-in) flat tin. Prick the base with a fork and line with foil. Bake for 10–15 minutes until set. Remove the foil and bake for a further 5–10 minutes until golden brown.

Whisk together the cream, coffee powder and sugar until thick. Spread the contents of the can, which is by now a toffee mixture, evenly over the base of the flan. Chop the banana and place evenly over the toffee then spread the cream mixture over the top. Chill before serving.

Chilled Vanilla Fruit Pudding

— ❦ —

This is a fairly heavy dessert which has the advantage of improving with age.
Not too long though – overnight is perfect.

Serves 6

50 g (2 oz) sponge cake, diced
25 g (1 oz) angelica, washed and
   diced
25 g (1 oz) glacé cherries
25 g (1 oz) sultanas
25 g (1 oz) currants

600 ml (1 pint) milk
1 vanilla pod
3 eggs
1 egg yolk
75 g (3 oz) sugar
Double cream, whipped, to serve

Butter 6 dariole moulds. Mix together the sponge and fruit and use to half
fill the moulds. Bring the milk and vanilla pod to the boil then remove from
the heat. Whisk together the eggs, egg yolk and sugar and pour the hot milk
onto the egg mixture. Remove the vanilla pod and whisk the egg and milk
mixture together.

Strain the custard into a jug and pour half into the dariole moulds. Leave to
stand for 10 minutes then fill to the top with the custard.

Stand the moulds in a roasting tin and fill with hot water to come halfway
up the sides of the moulds. Bake for 20–30 minutes until firm to touch.
Leave to chill. To serve, remove from the moulds and decorate with a little
whipped cream.

Crème Brûlée with Cointreau

This must be one of the simplest yet most luxurious puddings in the world. The art is getting the finish on the surface crunchy and not like concrete!

Serves 6–8

600 ml (1 pint) double cream
8 egg yolks
50 g (2 oz) caster sugar

Finely grated rind of ½ an orange
1 tablespoon cointreau
Soft brown sugar

Heat the cream in a pan, removing it from the heat just before it comes to the boil. Whisk the egg yolks and sugar together until the mixture is thick and pale in colour. Gradually add in the hot cream then the orange rind and cointreau. Place the bowl over a pan of simmering water and cook the custard over a low heat, stirring continuously, until it thickens. Pour the custard into individual ramekin dishes. Chill for 6 hours.

To serve, cover the top with an even layer of soft brown sugar. Place the dishes in a roasting tin with a little cold water (this will prevent the custard from curdling) and brown the sugar under a hot grill. Leave to cool before serving.

INDEX